WEIRD & WONDERFUL SCIENCE EXPERIMENTS

VOLUME 1

AT HOME

MoonDance

This library edition published in 2018 by MoonDance Press,
an imprint of The Quarto Group
6 Orchard Road, Suite 100
Lake Forest, CA 92630

Published by MoonDance Press,
a division of Quarto Publishing Group USA Inc.

Illustrations by Jeff Albrecht Studios
Cover and interior design by Melissa Gerber

Distributed in the United States and Canada by
Lerner Publisher Services
241 First Avenue North
Minneapolis, MN 55401 U.S.A.
www.lernerbooks.com

Printed in USA
9 8 7 6 5 4 3 2 1

MIX
Paper from
responsible sources
FSC® C008080

Contents

Introduction

Have you ever wanted to…
Fold an egg in half?
Make a snow cone in your kitchen?
Create your own bath bomb?

Naked Egg, page 26

Great! You'll find easy-to-follow instructions for these and so many more awesome at-home experiments in this book. No matter whether you set up your lab in the kitchen, the bathroom, or the backyard, you are guaranteed to have fun!

What's in this book?

- Many of the experiments can be done by kids all by themselves. That's right—no adult help needed. That means no grownups doing all the fun stuff while you watch. You can do lots of messy, cool, mind-blowing experiments all by yourself!

- All the supplies you need are probably already in your home. No fancy gadgets or doohickeys needed.

- Science is fun! There is no better boredom buster than a science experiment. You will learn something and astound and amaze your friends and family.

What are you waiting for?

Pick an experiment you are interested in, gather the materials, and get going! Make sure you check the safety instructions and find an adult to help if needed.

- **Supplies** includes all the stuff you need.

- **Do It!** has instructions for building and performing the experiment.

- **What's Happening?** Read the science behind the experiment.

- **What If?** includes ideas for making the experiment bigger, louder, longer, or just plain better.

Hot Chocolate Effect

This experiment is perfect for a cold morning, and you can drink it when you are done!

≡ Do It! ≡

Supplies

Ceramic mug, Instant hot chocolate mix, Hot water, Metal spoon

1. Tap the rim of the empty mug with your spoon and listen to the pitch (how high or low the sound is). Does it change?

2. Pour hot water into the mug and tap again. Any change?

3. Stir the water and tap the mug while the water is swirling. Any change now?

4. Pour a packet of hot chocolate into the mug. Stir it and tap again. You'll notice that the pitch gets higher. Stir and tap again. The pitch goes down and then rises again!

What's Happening?

Air bubbles are mixed into the liquid as you stir, which slow the speed of sound in the hot chocolate. This lowers the pitch of the sound that travels through the mug when tapped. As the water spins, the bubbles rise and pop. With fewer bubbles in the hot chocolate, the speed of sound and pitch increases.

Bendable Bones

Can you tie these bones in a knot? Can you tie them in a bow?

≡ Do It! ≡

Supplies

Clean chicken bones, Large jar, White vinegar

1. Put the bones in the jar and cover them with vinegar. Cover the jar with a lid.

2. Leave the jar on the counter for three days.

3. After three days, take the bones out of the jar. Can you bend them in knots? If not, stick the bones back in the jar, replace the vinegar, and wait another day or two before trying again.

What's Happening?

Bones contain minerals, mostly calcium and phosphorus, that make them strong and hard. Vinegar is a weak acid that scientists call acetic acid. The vinegar pulls out the minerals in the bone. All that's left is bendy, flexible cartilage.

Egg in a Bottle ADULT NEEDED

You may have seen a ship in a bottle, but have you ever put a whole egg in a bottle?

Supplies

Peeled hard-boiled egg, Glass bottle with an opening or neck smaller than the egg's diameter, Match, Sink

Do It!

1. The key to successfully getting the egg into the bottle is timing. Light a match and quickly drop it in the bottom of the bottle. The match should keep burning. If it goes out, drop in another lit match.

2. Count to three and put the egg on top of the bottle pointy side down so that it seals the opening.

3. Wait. After a few seconds, the egg will start to ooze down into the bottle.

What's Happening?

The burning match heats the air in the bottle, causing the air to expand. When you place the egg on top of the bottle, the match will go out as the oxygen burns up. The air cools and contracts so that the air pressure inside the bottle is much lower than the air pressure outside the bottle. The air outside of the bottle pushes the egg inside.

To get the egg out, reverse the process by making the air pressure inside the bottle greater than the air pressure outside so the air pushes the egg back out again. Here are two ways to do this:

The Easy Way

Turn the bottle downward at an angle. Shake it around a little until the egg is in the neck of the bottle and covers it completely with the pointy side pointed outward. Make sure there aren't any match bits in the way. Then bring the bottle to the sink, and let hot water run over the bottom of the bottle. This will heat the air inside the bottle so that it expands and pushes the egg out.

The Fun (Messy) Way

Try this method outdoors. Add two effervescent tablets to the bottle and ½ cup of water. Quickly turn the bottle upside down so that the egg is in the neck of the bottle with the pointy side pointed downward. As the tablets bubble in the water, they produce carbon dioxide gas, which builds up the air pressure inside the bottle very quickly and shoots the egg out.

What If?

What if you use very hot water instead of a match?

Straw Through a Potato

Here's one way to prove your superhuman strength!

Supplies

Straw, Potato

Do It!

1. Place your thumb over the end of the straw.
2. Stab the potato, and watch the straw go right through. Just watch out that your hand isn't on the other side or the potato won't be the only thing with a hole!

What's Happening?

A plastic straw is pretty weak. If you try to jam it into the potato without covering the end of the straw, the straw will bend before it even pierces the skin. By trapping the air inside with your thumb, you strengthen the straw so that it can't bend. As the straw goes through the potato, it just gets stronger because the air inside is compressed when the other end fills up with potato!

Drink a Rainbow

Rainbows aren't just for unicorns. Try this colorful density column experiment you can drink!

Supplies

Tall glass, A variety of juices, Water, Blue food coloring, Measuring cup, Syringe (optional)

Do It!

1. Pour a cup of water into the glass and add a few drops of blue food coloring.
2. Pour ¼ cup of one juice into the glass.
3. With a syringe or measuring cup, carefully pour in ¼ cup of another juice so it runs down the inside of the glass. If the new juice sinks below the first juice, it is denser than the first. If it floats on top, it is less dense.
4. Continue with the rest of the juices and water until you have a layered rainbow of juice.

What's Happening?

A layering of liquids like this is called a density column. Density is a measure of how much stuff (or mass) is in a set volume. In this demonstration, the volume is ¼ cup. The mass depends on the sugar and other stuff that is in the juice. The juices with a higher density sink to the bottom, and the juices with lower density float on top. The layers form when you slowly introduce the juices by pouring them on the inside of the glass, so they don't mix with each other.

Taste with Your Eyes

Can you trick your taste buds with food coloring?

Do It!

1. Pour some juice into the four cups.
2. Add food coloring to three of the cups so that one is orange, one is red, one is green, and one stays clear. Don't let your volunteers see!
3. Show the first volunteer the glasses of juice. Ask them to predict each flavor, and write their answer.
4. Let the volunteer taste each of the drinks. Ask what flavor they taste, and rate them from most to least sweet. Write this down, as well.
5. Repeat with each of your volunteers. Did the predictions match what they tasted? Did anyone realize that the juices all have the same flavor?

What's Happening?

We associate color with certain flavors. With sweet food, red usually means cherry, orange color means orange flavor, and green means lime. What we see can override what we think we taste.

Taste with Your Nose

Have you smelled a meal so good you could taste it? Your sense of smell is a big part of how food tastes.

Do It!

1. Put each flavor jellybean in a plastic bag and squish them. Make sure you have twice as many jellybeans of each flavor as volunteers.
2. Have your first volunteer wear a nose plug and a blindfold.
3. Give them a jellybean to eat. Write down the answer they tell you next to the correct flavor. Repeat this for all three flavors.
4. Remove the nose plug but leave the blindfold on. Ask your volunteer to smell each bag and identify the flavor by smell.
5. Let the volunteer smell and taste the jellybeans and ask them to identify the flavor.
6. Repeat this for each volunteer.

What's Happening?

Much of the flavor of food comes from the thousands of receptors in your nose. When your sense of smell is blocked, it is more difficult to taste flavors.

Better with Butter

The best butter is the kind you make yourself.

Supplies

Measuring cup, Large cup, 3 cups of heavy whipping cream, Clean glass jar with a lid, Stopwatch, Bowl, Water, Sealable container for storing your butter

Do It!

1. Pour 1½ cups of cream into the large cup, and let it sit on the counter until it is room temperature. While you're waiting, start making butter with the cold cream.

2. Pour ½ cup of cream straight from the fridge into the glass jar. Put the lid tightly on the jar, start your stopwatch, and start shaking vigorously. You will need to shake the jar for up to 20 minutes (or more!), so it helps to have a friend who will take turns with you.

3. After 5 to 20 minutes, the solid parts of the cream will separate from the liquid parts. When you have a solid yellow lump in a jar of watery buttermilk, stop shaking (and stop the stopwatch).

4. Take the yellow butter blob out of the jar and put it in a bowl of clean water. Rinse the butter and squish as much of the liquid out as you can. Pour out the water and rinse the butter at least two more times. This will keep your butter from turning rancid before you can eat it.

5. Once your butter is well rinsed, put it in the sealable container and store it in the fridge.

6. Make six batches of butter—three using the cold butter and three using the room temperature butter. Clean the jar in between each batch. Which temperature cream made butter faster? Is there a difference in the color, texture, or taste of the butters?

What's Happening?

When you shake cream, the fat bounces around and clumps together, eventually clumping so much that the buttery fat separates completely from the liquid in the cream. Warm molecules bounce around faster because they have more energy. The molecules in the room-temperature cream are warmer and already bouncing faster than the ones in the chilled cream. This means the room-temperature fat molecules will clump together and form butter faster.

What If?

What if you put a marble in the glass jar with the cream? Does it speed up the process?

Ice Cream in a Bag

Do the ice cream dance!

Supplies

1 gallon freezer bag, 1 quart freezer bag, 1 cup half-and-half, 2 tablespoons sugar, 1 teaspoon vanilla extract, Ice, ½ cup rock salt, Thermometer, Gloves

What's Happening?

Plain ice both melts and re-freezes. When you add salt to the bag, more energy is needed to melt the salty ice. The salty ice pulls that energy from the warmer bag of ice cream, making it colder.

Do It!

1. Pour the half-and-half, sugar, and vanilla into the smaller freezer bag. Seal the bag so there is little extra air inside.
2. Fill the larger freezer bag half full of ice. Record the temperature of the ice in the bag.
3. Add the rock salt to the ice.
4. Place the smaller bag with the ice cream mixture in the larger bag of ice and salt. Seal the large bag.
5. Put on gloves and shake the bags for 10 to 15 minutes.
6. When the ice cream is solid, remove it from the larger bag. Measure and record the temperature of the ice left in the larger bag. What happened to the temperature of the ice as you shook the bag?

The Gelatin Jiggle

What fruits make a gelatin that jiggles instead of a mushy mess?

Supplies

4 packages of cherry sugar-free gelatin, 4 large bowls, 1 peach, 1 can of peaches, 1 can of pineapple, 1 pineapple, Knife, Pot, Measuring cup, Clock

ADULT NEEDED

Do It!

1. Cut the fruit into bite-sized pieces. Measure 1 cup of each of the four fruits.
2. Prepare 4 bowls of gelatin by following the directions on the box.
3. Add a different fruit to each bowl and label each of the bowls.
4. Refrigerate the bowls.
5. Every 10 minutes, touch the gelatin. When no gelatin sticks to your finger, the gelatin is set. Write down the time.
6. Which fruit took the longest to set? The fastest? Did any fruits never set?

What's Happening?

Fruits contain enzymes, chemicals that help them grow and ripen. Some fruits contain an enzyme that digests gelatin. If you add a fruit with this enzyme, the gelatin won't set. However, canning or cooking the fruit destroys this enzyme. Which fruits contain the gelatin-eating enzyme?

Make Meringue

This easy dessert requires a lot of arm power, so roll up your sleeves and give those egg whites what for.

Supplies

12 room temperature eggs, 4 cups of sugar, Measuring cup, Stopwatch, Whisk, Glass bowl, Plastic bowl, Copper bowl, Spoon, Parchment paper (optional), Baking sheet, Oven

Do It!

1. Preheat your oven to 225°F.
2. Crack two of the eggs, and pour just the egg whites into the glass bowl.
3. Start your stopwatch, and begin to briskly whisk the eggs.
4. After a minute or so, the eggs will become foamy. Keep whisking while gradually adding ⅔ cup of sugar.
5. After several more minutes of whisking, the eggs should become stiff and shiny. If you lift the whisk out of the eggs, a peak should form that doesn't fall down. Stop your stopwatch when this happens and record the time.
6. Place a piece of parchment paper on your baking sheet. Scoop the egg whites onto the baking sheet with a spoon, placing them 1 inch apart.
7. Put the baking sheet in the oven and bake for 90 minutes. Remove the meringues before they turn brown, and let them cool completely before eating.
8. Repeat this two times for each bowl. Which type of bowl took the longest to whip the meringues? Were there differences in color or consistency?

What's Happening?

Egg whites are made of 90 percent water and some protein. When you first crack the egg, the egg white proteins are wrapped around the water. As you beat the egg whites with a whisk, you unwrap the proteins and add a whole lot of air bubbles. The unwrapped proteins realign to form a net that holds the air bubbles in place. As you bake the meringue, the air evaporates, leaving a tasty protein shell.

So why does it matter which bowl you use? The tiniest bit of oil or grease can keep the proteins from realigning to make big, fluffy clouds. Oil and fats stick to plastic bowls and are pretty much impossible to remove completely when cleaning. So unless your plastic bowl is brand new, odds are a tiny bit of oil got in your meringue. Copper bowls help meringues even more. A tiny bit of copper from the surface of the bowl gets mixed into the egg whites and stabilizes them, making it easier for them to hold in all those air bubbles.

Yeasty Beasties

Those tiny holes in a slice of bread are bubbles made by the burps of billions of tiny fungi called yeast. Harness their gas to blow up balloons.

Supplies

5 identical empty bottles, Warm water, Measuring cup, 5 packets of baker's yeast, Sugar, Sucralose, Corn syrup, Honey, 5 balloons

Do It!

1. Blow up each balloon three times. Label each bottle with a different sweetener. One bottle will not have a sweetener.
2. Pour ½ cup of warm water into each bottle, and then add a packet of yeast to each.
3. Add a tablespoon of sweetener to each bottle matching its label.
4. Swirl the bottles gently to mix the contents. Put a balloon on the top of each bottle. Wait an hour. Which balloon is the biggest? Which inflated the fastest?

What's Happening?

As the dry yeast is brought back to life by the water and eats the sugar, it releases carbon dioxide gas. The gas fills the bottle and then fills the balloon. Which of the sugars in your experiment was the best food for the yeasty beasties?

Gluten Goodness

Why are some breads light and fluffy, while others are dense and chewy? The magic ingredient is gluten.

Do It!

Supplies

Whole-wheat flour, Bread flour, All-purpose flour, Pastry flour, Water, 4 bowls, Measuring cup, Measuring tape

1. Pour 1 cup of whole-wheat flour in a bowl, and add ¾ cup of water.
2. Mix the flour and water until you have a soft, rubbery ball.
3. Measure the ball, and then let it rest on the counter for 10 minutes.
4. Run cold water over the ball in the sink. Squeeze it to remove the starch. You will see the white starch dissolving in the water. Stop when the water runs clear and the ball is a sticky web of gluten strands. Now the ball is pure gluten.
5. Measure your gluten ball. Has the size changed? How does it feel, stretch, look, and bounce?
6. Repeat the process with the other flours. Which flour had the biggest change in size when you removed the starch?

What's Happening?

When bread rises, the yeast in the dough makes gas. The stretchy gluten in the flour fills with gas like a balloon. More gluten means more and bigger "balloons" in the bread, making the bread more light and fluffy.

Fruity DNA Extraction

All living things have one thing in common: DNA!

Supplies

Rubbing alcohol (70% or greater), 3 strawberries, Sealable plastic bag, 2 clear glasses, Water, Dish soap, Salt, Half a banana, Kiwi, Measuring cup, Coffee filter, Skewer

≡ Do It! ≡

1. Put the rubbing alcohol in the freezer.
2. Pull the leaves off the strawberries, and put them in the plastic bag. Push all of the air out of the bag and seal it tight.
3. Mash the strawberries until you have a slimy mess.
4. In one of the glasses, pour 1 cup of water, 4 teaspoons of soap, and 1 teaspoon of salt. Stir the mixture gently so you don't make bubbles.
5. Open the bag of strawberries and pour ⅓ cup of the soap-salt mixture in with the fruit. Push the air out of the bag and seal it. Gently squish the bag for 30 seconds until blended. Let the bag sit for 20 minutes.
6. Put a coffee filter over the other glass so that the center is in the glass and the sides are folded over.

7. Pour the fruit mixture into the coffee filter. Squeeze out the liquid into the glass, careful not to tear the filter.
8. When you've squeezed out all the liquid you can, carefully pour the rubbing alcohol down the side of the glass. The alcohol layer on top should be as thick as the juice layer.
9. After a few seconds, you will see a white cloudy layer form between the fruit and the alcohol. This is the DNA! After 10 minutes, it will rise to the top of the alcohol layer. If you aren't that patient, poke the tip of the skewer into the middle of that layer. Gently twist the stick so that the DNA wraps around it, and pull it out of the glass.
10. Repeat the process with the kiwi and half a banana. Which fruit produced the most DNA?

What's Happening?

To take the DNA out of the cell, first you must break open the cells. When you squished up the fruit, you broke up the cells. The soap in the extraction solution destroys the rest of the cell walls and the membrane of the nucleus, letting out the DNA. The salt in the solution causes the proteins and carbohydrates that make up the rest of the cell to sink to the bottom while the DNA stays on top. Next, you filtered out most of the other plant parts so you are left with DNA dissolved in water. Adding cold rubbing alcohol to the mixture simply increases the amount of DNA you are able to separate from the rest of the cell parts. Because different plants (and animals, for that matter) have different amounts of DNA, how much you can extract from each plant should vary in the same way.

Get the Iron Out

It turns out that most cereals contain the same iron found in nails. See it with your own eyes!

Supplies

3 types of cereals with different iron contents, 2 tall glasses, Measuring cup, Plastic spoon, Strong magnet (neodymium magnets work best), Clear packing tape, Plastic sandwich bag, Camera or paper and pencil

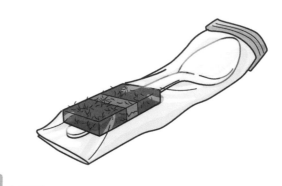

Do It!

1. Pour 1 cup of one cereal into a tall glass.
2. Fill the cup with water so that it is about an inch above the cereal.
3. Let the glass sit for at least five minutes so the cereal gets good and soggy.
4. Put the strong magnet in the corner of the plastic bag so it is tight around the magnet.
5. Tape the magnet onto the end of the handle of the spoon so some of it hangs off the end and the bag is sealed. Cut off the rest of the bag. This is your magnetic stirrer.
6. Fill the second glass with clean water.
7. Stir the cereal soup with the magnetic stirrer (the magnet should be inside in the soup) for about two minutes.
8. Gently rinse off your stirrer and take a look at the magnet. You should see black particles sticking to the magnet. This is the iron from the breakfast cereal.
9. Take a photo or make a drawing so that you can compare the amount of iron in the different cereals. Repeat this for the other two cereals. If you can, repeat more than once for each cereal. Which cereal did you remove the most and least iron from? Does this match the iron contents on the cereal labels?

What's Happening?

Your body needs iron to survive. Red blood cells use iron to carry oxygen from your lungs to the rest of your body. Because some people don't get enough iron from foods like red meat and green leafy vegetables, iron is added to foods like cereal. The iron powder used in these foods is the same iron used to make nails!

Just like with a nail, bringing a magnet near the cereal attracts the iron. In fact, if you float a single piece of cereal in a bowl of water and your magnet is strong enough, you can move the cereal around the bowl by moving the magnet in the air above it.

What If?

What if you try this experiment on other iron-fortified foods, such as baby food, energy bars, or vitamin supplements?

Drink Your Iron

When you don't have enough iron in your body, you feel tired and get sick more easily. A delicious way to get iron is through fruit juice!

Supplies

Pitcher, 3 tea bags, 6 clear glasses, 6 spoons, Measuring spoon, Masking tape and marker, Pineapple juice, White grape juice, Prune juice, Cranberry juice, Apple juice

Do It!

1. Pour a pint of hot water into the pitcher and add three tea bags. Let the pitcher sit for an hour.
2. Pour ¼ cup of each juice into a different glass. (One glass will have no juice.) Label each glass.
3. Add ¼ cup of tea to each glass and stir each with a spoon. Let it sit for 20 minutes.
4. Lift each glass and look for dark particles on the bottom.
5. Let the tea mixtures sit for another two hours, and then look for dark iron particles again. Which juice produced the most particles? Does the number of particles correspond to the iron content of the juices?

What's Happening?

Tea is full of chemicals called polyphenols, which give tea its flavor and provide health benefits. Some of those polyphenols also react with iron in foods, like fruit juice, and form solids that sink to the bottom of the glass.

Clearing Up Cola

Sometimes mixing drinks leads to deliciousness, but pouring milk in your cola leads to something surprising and a little gross.

Do It!

Supplies

Small clear bottle of cola, 2% milk

1. Remove the label from the bottle of cola so that you can see the experiment easily.
2. Open the cola and pour in some milk so that the liquid is just an inch from the top. Put the lid back on the bottle and watch. The changes may take up to an hour.

What's Happening?

After about 15 minutes, you will see dark, foamy clumps near the bottom of the bottle. The phosphoric acid in the cola is reacting with casein protein in the milk, causing it to clump with caramel coloring and other parts of the soda. After an hour, the bottom will be full of the dark, curdled milk. The clear top layer is the water, sweetener, and the rest of the proteins and fat from the milk. Let the bottle of cola sit overnight. When you wake up, it should be completely clear!

Ripening Fruit

When you're faced with a hard pear, ripen it with science!

Do It!

Supplies

4 unripe pears,
2 ripe bananas,
3 paper lunch
bags, Marker,
Masking tape

1. With the marker, label the bags: "Pear," "Pear & Banana," and "Pear & 2 Bananas."
2. Place the fruit in the bags, and seal them with tape. Leave the last pear on the counter.
3. Keep track of the date and time you put the fruit in the bags. Every 12 hours, check the pears' ripeness by pressing on the side of the pear firmly with your finger for two seconds. If the fruit stays indented after you remove your finger, then it is ripe. If you cannot see where you pressed, put the fruit back and reseal the bag. Check the pear on the counter too.
4. Note when each pear ripens. Did the pears in the bag ripen before the one on the counter? Did the bananas help the pears ripen faster?

What's Happening?

Have you ever heard the saying "one rotten apple will spoil the bunch"? Long ago, apples were stored in large barrels in cool cellars so they could be eaten year-round. An over-ripe apple in the barrel would give off a chemical called ethylene that caused the apples to ripen too quickly and rot before they were eaten. Here, the ethylene given off by the bananas caused the pears to ripen sooner. The ethylene molecule is too big to escape from the paper bag. Oxygen — which keeps the fruit from rotting — can flow freely in and out of the bag.

Floating Fruit

It's the citrus Olympics! Which fruit will float above the rest?

Do It!

Supplies

2 oranges, 2 limes,
2 lemons, Large
bowl of water

1. Peel the rind off of one orange, one lemon, and one lime. Leave the other fruits unpeeled.
2. Put all the fruit in the bowl of water and watch what happens. Which fruits float and which fruits sink? Do any hang out in the middle?

What's Happening?

Juicy fruits like oranges and lemons are mostly juice on the inside, which has a density about the same as water. But the rinds have pockets of air and act like little life jackets. Limes are different. If you cut the fruit in half, you'll see that the lime has a lot more pulp and a denser flesh than oranges and lemons. This makes the lime denser and weighs it down in the water, even with the rind on.

Mayo Emulsion

When a bottle of vinaigrette dressing sits for awhile, the oil and vinegar separate into two layers. Even if you shake the bottle as hard as you can, the oil and vinegar will always separate – that is, unless you make an emulsion!

Supplies

Vegetable oil, Water, White vinegar, 2 small bowls, Fork, Egg, Mustard powder, Sugar, Flour, Pint-sized glass jar with cover, Measuring cup, Measuring spoon, Magnifying glass

Do It!

1. Pour ¼ cup of water and ¼ cup of vegetable oil into the jar, and put the cover on tightly.
2. Shake the jar as hard as you can for one minute to mix the oil and water completely.
3. Let the jar sit for five minutes and observe what happens, using the magnifying glass to look closely as the two liquids separate.
4. Separate the egg white and yolk into the two small bowls and then use a fork to beat each of them until they are smooth.
5. Open the jar and add the egg yolk to the oil and water.
6. Shake the jar as hard as you can for three minutes so the oil and water are completely mixed.
7. Let the jar sit for five minutes and observe what happens with the magnifying glass. Do the oil and water separate this time?
8. Clean out your jar and add another ¼ cup of water and ¼ of vegetable oil, and then add the egg white to the jar, as well.
9. Shake the jar as hard as you can for three minutes until the oil and water are completely mixed.
10. Let the jar sit for five minutes and observe what happens with the magnifying glass. Do the oil and water separate this time?
11. Repeat this process three more times with a tablespoon of mustard powder, a tablespoon of sugar, and a tablespoon of flour. Which additives kept the oil and water from separating?

What's Happening?

Oil and water don't mix because the water molecules stick to each other more than they stick to the oil. The oil will float on top because it's less dense than the water. However, when you add an emulsifier to the mixture, the water and oil will stay mixed up. The emulsifier sticks equally to water and oil, so it surrounds tiny droplets of each and lets them hang out together. We call this stable mixture of oil and water an emulsion.

Apple Exposure

Can you stop the oxidation process that makes apple slices turn brown?

ADULT NEEDE

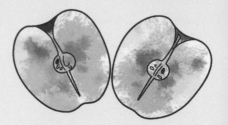

Supplies

4 apples, Knife, 6 bowls, Masking tape, Marker, Measuring cup, Water, Lemon juice, Salt, Lemon-lime soda, Honey, Carbonated water, Resealable bag

Do It!

1. Put one liquid in each of the bowls. One bowl will be empty. Label the bowls.
   • 1 cup of carbonated water
   • 1 cup of lemon-lime soda
   • 1 cup of water + 1 tablespoon of lemon juice
   • 1 cup of water + ⅛ teaspoon of salt
   • 1 cup of water + 2 tablespoons of honey

2. Cut the apples into eight slices. Put four slices in each of the bowls and four more in a resealable bag, sealing it tight.

3. After five minutes, pour out the liquids, and wait for one hour. Did any of the apple slices turn brown? How about the slices in the empty bowl? Which liquid kept the apples white longest?

4. Taste the apples. Do any taste different?

What's Happening?

When a cut apple is exposed to oxygen in the air, it reacts with the apple's enzymes to make it brown. This is called oxidation. Weak acids (lemon juice, soda, salt water, and carbonated water) slow the reaction. Honey and the resealable bag keep the air away from the apple.

One Plus One

Dissolve sugar into water and see how things add up... or don't!

Do It!

1. Place tape on the side of the jar from top to bottom.
2. Pour 1 cup of water into the jar. Label the water line on the tape 1 cup.
3. Pour in another cup of water. Label the water line 2 cups.
4. Empty the jar and dry it.
5. Pour 1 cup of sugar into the jar, and then 1 cup of water. Mix. What is the level?
6. Add sugar ¼ cup at a time until it reaches the 2-cup level. How much sugar did you add to make 2 cups of solution?

Supplies

Clear quart jar, Water, Measuring cup, 1 cup of sugar, Masking tape, Marker

What's Happening?

The sugar dissolves, but the air in the spaces between the sugar grains does not. When you pour the sugar into the water, the air isn't poured in. Even though you mixed 1 cup of water plus 1 cup of sugar, you still get less than 2 cups of sugar water.

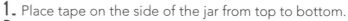

Salty Science

ADULT NEEDED

Common wisdom says to add salt to water when you cook because it makes the food cook more quickly. Does a pinch of salt really make a difference? How about a whole cup of salt?

Supplies

Small sauce pan, Stove top, Measuring cup, Measuring spoon, Water, Table salt, Food thermometer

Do It!

1. Pour 4 cups of water into the pan and place it on the stove.
2. Turn the burner on high and wait for the water to come to a complete boil.
3. Carefully measure the water's temperature, and then turn off the burner.
4. Once the water has stopped boiling, add 1 tablespoon of water and 2 tablespoons of salt.
5. Turn the burner on high and wait for the water to come to a boil again.
6. Measure the temperature of the water, and then turn off the burner.
7. Repeat the process as you continue to add salt to the water, doubling the amount of salt in the water each time, and adding 1 tablespoon of water each time to make up for the water that has evaporated during boiling.
8. The last time you measure the boiling point, the pot will be half water and half salt. What happened to the boiling point as you added salt? How hot do you think the water would boil if you doubled the salt again? Did you notice anything about how long it took the salty water to come to a boil?

What's Happening?

When you heat water, you are giving the molecules energy so they can move around faster. If you add enough heat, the water molecules can break free of the liquid water to become a gas and the water starts boiling. The bubbles in the boiling water are those fast-moving molecules that broke free from the liquid water.

When you add salt, it takes more energy for the molecules to break free. Salt is a crystal called sodium chloride, but when you add it to water, the sodium and chlorine in the salt break apart. The water molecules stick to the sodium and the chlorine more than they stick to each other, so it takes more energy to break free of the liquid. More energy is more heat and more heat is a higher temperature! Therefore, when you add salt to water, you have to heat (or energize) the water more before it starts to boil.

Use Your Noodle

Boiling a lot of water before you put noodles in a pot takes a long time. Try some not-so-common ways of cooking noodles to see if you can save time and energy.

Supplies

Five 1-pound boxes of elbow macaroni, Water, Pot, Slotted spoon, Colander, Stopwatch

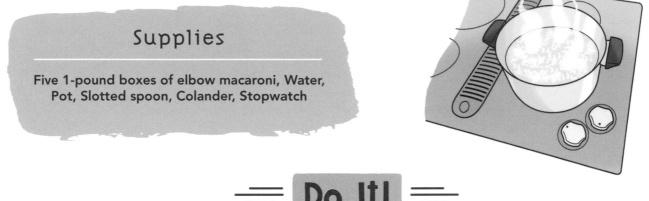

Do It!

1. Cook each of the five boxes of noodles using each method below. For each method, time how long you heat the water using the stove and the total time it takes to cook the noodles.

2. For methods 1 to 4: While the noodles cook, use a slotted spoon to take the noodles out and taste if fully cooked every minute. The noodles are fully cooked when they are soft but not crunchy and not mushy.

   - Method 1: Put 4 quarts of cold water in the pot. Turn on the stove. When the water is at a full boil, add the noodles. Turn off the stove when the noodles are cooked.

   - Method 2: Put 2 quarts of cold water in the pot. Turn on the stove. When the water is at a full boil, add the noodles. Turn off the stove when the noodles are cooked.

   - Method 3: Put 2 quarts of cold water in the pot and pour in the noodles. Turn on the stove. Turn off the stove when the noodles are cooked.

   - Method 4: Put 2 quarts of cold water in the pot and pour in the noodles. Let the noodles soak in the water until they are cooked.

   - Method 5: Put 2 quarts of cold water in the pot. Turn on the stove. When the water is at a full boil, add the noodles. Turn off the stove and cover the pot. Check the noodles every minute after 10 minutes. Only remove the lid briefly to remove a noodle to taste.

   Which method cooked the noodles the quickest? Which used the least energy (the stove was on for the shortest amount of time)? Was there any difference in the taste of the noodles?

What's Happening?

The first step in cooking dry noodles — which are made of starch and protein — is to get them wet. The starch absorbs the water until it bursts. The starch inside the noodles gradually soaks up water, making the noodle softer. The proteins also begin to cook, keeping the noodles from turning into a total starchy mush. The noodle is perfectly cooked when the starches are wet and the protein is cooked but not so much that it falls apart. Do you really need all that water, and does it need to boil to properly cook the noodles all the way through?

Hot Water Freeze

Hot water sometimes freezes faster than cold water, and scientists are not completely sure why. See if you can figure it out!

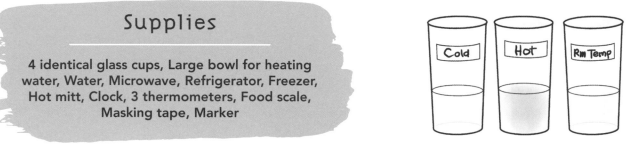

ADULT NEEDED

Supplies

4 identical glass cups, Large bowl for heating water, Water, Microwave, Refrigerator, Freezer, Hot mitt, Clock, 3 thermometers, Food scale, Masking tape, Marker

Do It!

1. Measure ½ cup of water into two of the cups.
2. Label one cup "Cold," and place it in the refrigerator.
3. Label the other cup "Room Temperature," and place it on the counter.
4. Wait 15 minutes for the temperature of the waters to match their location.
5. Measure ½ cup of water into the third cup, and mark the top of the water with tape. Label this cup "Hot." Pour ½ cup of water in the last cup, and put both of these cups in the microwave. Heat the water for one to two minutes or until the water is steaming.
6. Remove the water from the microwave. If the water in the third cup is below the level marked by the tape, pour in some of the extra hot water from the last cup so that it is back to the ½ cup level.

7. Place a thermometer in each cup, and record their temperatures. Place the labeled cups in the freezer. Make sure they are all on the same level and none of the cups are touching anything in the freezer.
8. Measure the temperature of the water in each container every five minutes. Keep the freezer door closed as much as possible. Once the temperature of the water reaches 32°F/0°C, stop taking temperatures. Continue to observe the water every five minutes to see which forms ice crystals first.
9. Which cup of water reached the freezing temperature first? Which actually froze first? If the hot water did not freeze first, can you change some of the conditions so that it does?

What's Happening?

Nobody can really explain what happens here. Some scientists observe that the hot water freezes before the cold water, and others do not. All agree that sometimes the hot water does freeze fast, but no one is sure of the conditions that allow this to happen or why it happens. Now known as the Mpemba Effect — named after a high school student in Tanzania who was the first to scientifically study the effect — hot water freezing more quickly than cold water was observed as far back as Aristotle and has been written about by several scientists since then.

Upside-down Toast

When you drop your buttered toast, why does it land butter-side down?

Supplies

Toast, Aluminum foil, Measuring tape, Low table, Books

Do It!

1. Wrap one side of the toast with foil. This simulates the weight of butter.
2. Measure the height of your table, and then slide your toast off the table edge.
3. Record what side your toast landed on. If the toast flipped when it landed, it landed on an edge. Repeat six times.
4. Place a book on the edge of your table so that the surface is at least 4 inches taller. Drop your toast six times from this new height.
5. Continuing adding height and dropping the toast until you reach 48 inches. At which heights did your toast land butter-side down? How about butter-side up?

What's Happening?

As the toast slides off the edge, one side starts to fall before the rest, causing the toast to spin. If the table is high enough, the toast will rotate completely and land butter-side up. If the table is too low, there will not be enough time for the toast to spin all the way around and it will land butter-side down.

Potatosmosis

Spuds and salt come together for this fascinating experiment.

Supplies

4 small bowls, Measuring cup, Measuring spoon, Salt, Masking tape, Marker, 2 large potatoes, Peeler, Knife, Kitchen scale

Do It!

1. Pour 1 cup of water in the first bowl. In the second bowl, mix 1 cup of water and 1 tablespoon of salt. In the third bowl, mix 1 cup of water and 4 tablespoons of salt. Leave the last bowl empty. Label each bowl.
2. Peel the potatoes, and cut them into 12 1-inch squares.
3. Weigh the pieces three at a time on the scale, and write down their weights. Put three pieces in each bowl.
4. Let the potatoes soak for 30 minutes.
5. Weigh the pieces. Compare the before and after weights. Which solutions caused the potatoes to gain or lose weight?

What's Happening?

When water moves in and out of a plant cell wall, we call that osmosis. Osmosis is a type of diffusion, which is the movement from high to low concentration. Here, the water moves from high concentration in the potato to low concentration in the salt water, causing the potato to lose weight.

Curds & Whey

I'm not entirely sure what a tuffet is or why Miss Muffet was sitting on one, but in this experiment, you can make your own curds and whey. Just keep an eye out for spiders.

Supplies

Jar or small bowl, Cheesecloth, Rubber band, 1 cup skim milk, 1 tablespoon lemon juice, Measuring spoon, Measuring cup, Metal saucepan, Stove or hot plate, Kitchen scale, Whole milk, Half-and-half

═ Do It! ═

1. Create a strainer by placing three layers of cheesecloth over a jar or small bowl and securing it with a rubber band.

2. Pour 1 cup of skim milk into the saucepan.

3. Heat the milk on the stove until you see steam rising off the top. Be careful not to boil the milk.

4. Stir in 1 tablespoon of lemon juice.

5. Heat the milk until you see solids separate from the liquid. The solids are curds and the liquid is whey.

6. Turn off the heat, and carefully pour your curds and whey through the strainer to separate them. Let the curds drain for at least two minutes.

7. Take the cheesecloth off the strainer, and squeeze out the rest of the whey.

8. Observe the curds. What color are they? How wet are they? What is the texture when you squeeze the curds in your hand?

9. Use the kitchen scale to weigh the curds made from skim milk. Then you can even taste the curds and whey (a little salt might help).

10. Clean up your supplies, and repeat the process for the whole milk and half-and-half. Which kind of milk made the most curds? How did the curds' color, texture, and taste compare?

What's Happening?

A glass of milk is mostly made of water. In the water are tiny bits of proteins, lactose, and fat mixed so smoothly that you can't see them. In this experiment, you separated the curds (solids) from the whey (liquids). This happens because of a protein in milk called casein.

Casein carries minerals like calcium and phosphorus to the cells in your body. In a regular glass of milk, the casein proteins repel each other. But when you add an acid like lemon juice, they change shape and stick together, gathering lactose and fats along the way in solid chunks called curds. The water and the rest of the proteins and fats are left behind in the whey.

Cook an Egg

You don't actually need a stove to cook an egg. Just don't try to eat these!

Supplies

Raw egg, Bowl, Rubbing alcohol

*Wash your hands with soap after handling raw eggs

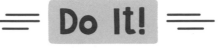

Do It!

1. Pour rubbing alcohol into the bowl.
2. Crack the egg into the bowl of rubbing alcohol. What happens to the egg?
3. Check on the egg every 10 minutes. How does it change? After about one hour, the egg should be completely "cooked."

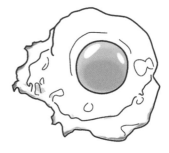

What's Happening?

When you cook an egg with heat, the proteins in the egg white become denatured. This means it loses its regular shape and gets tangled up with other proteins in the egg. This causes the egg whites to change from a clear liquid to a white solid. Alcohol does pretty much the same thing to the proteins in the egg white, using a chemical reaction instead of heat.

Spinning Eggs

Have you ever wondered how to tell a raw egg from a hard-boiled egg without breaking the shell? Just give the eggs a spin!

Supplies

Raw egg, Hard-boiled egg

Do It!

1. Let both eggs sit out on the counter for 15 minutes so they are room temperature.
2. Spin the eggs on their side one at a time. Do the eggs spin in the same way?

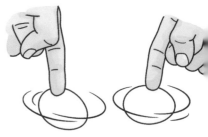

What's Happening?

The insides of raw egg are liquid, but a hard-boiled egg is solid. When you spin a raw egg, its center of gravity changes as the liquid inside the egg moves around, causing a wobbly spin. When you spin a hard-boiled egg, the solid center has a fixed center of gravity, giving a smooth, balanced spin.

Egg Toss

Throw eggs at a target – all in the name of science!

Supplies

Raw eggs, 2 sheets, 2 friends

* Be sure to wash your hands with soap after handling raw eggs to prevent the spread of bacterial diseases like salmonella.

Do It!

1. Have your two friends hold the sheet up flat against a wall (preferably outside, in case you miss!).

2. Stand back about 3 feet from the wall and throw an egg as hard as you can at the sheet. What happens when the egg hits the wall?

3. Now have your two friends hold the other sheet up in an open area outside.

4. Have them hold the top of the sheet up high and the bottom of the sheet up and out a bit so the sheet hangs loosely and the bottom makes a curve, like the letter "J."

5. Stand back about 3 feet and throw an egg as hard as you can at the sheet. What happens when the egg hits the sheet?

What's Happening?

When you throw an egg at a wall, it smashes into a mess! But when you throw an egg at the curved sheet, the egg doesn't even crack. The difference in these two cases is the change in momentum, called impulse.

Momentum is mass multiplied by speed. Because the mass of the eggs is about the same, what matters is the speed. The change in momentum for the egg is about the same in both cases: it goes from moving very fast to stopping completely.

But the time it takes to stop in each case is totally different. Impulse, or change in momentum, is the force the egg feels, multiplied by the amount of time it feels that force.

When the egg hits the wall, the time to stop is very small. This means the force is very large — large enough to smash the egg! But when you throw the egg against the sheet, the time to stop is much longer, so the force is much smaller, and the egg is unbroken.

What If?

What if you stand closer to or farther from the sheet? What if your friends hold the sheet very tightly?

Floating Eggs

Do eggs float or sink? In this experiment, they do both at the same time!

Supplies

Tall clear glass, Raw egg, Water, Salt, Measuring spoon, Stirring

Do It!

1. Fill the glass with enough water to cover the egg. Put the egg in the glass. Does it float?
2. Add 1 tablespoon of salt to the water, and give it a gentle stir. Does the egg float now?
3. Keep adding salt, 1 tablespoon at a time. How much salt causes the egg to start floating? How much salt causes the egg to float to the top of the water?
4. Once the egg floats at the top, pour in fresh water. Where does the egg float now?

What's Happening?

An egg is denser than water, so it sinks to the bottom of the glass. Adding salt increases the water's density. When the egg lifts off the bottom of the glass, the density of the egg and salt water are about the same. When the egg floats at the top, the salt water is much denser than the egg. The salt water is so dense that the fresh water you add to the glass just floats on the salty water. The egg is floating on the salt water and sinking in the fresh water at the same time!

Naked Egg

Turn a raw egg into a "naked" egg with this overnight trick!

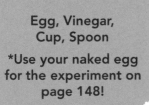

Supplies

Egg, Vinegar, Cup, Spoon

*Use your naked egg for the experiment on page 148!

Do It!

1. Put the egg in the cup, and pour vinegar into the cup until the egg is completely covered.
2. Wait 24 hours, and then carefully pour the vinegar out and add fresh vinegar to cover the egg again. Wait another 24 hours or until the eggshell is completely dissolved.
3. Rinse off the egg. You now have a naked, bouncy egg! Be careful: The egg membrane will break if you bounce the egg too hard.

What's Happening?

The shell of an egg is mostly made of calcium carbonate. Vinegar reacts with the calcium carbonate to make water, calcium acetate, and carbon dioxide gas. Did you notice all those carbon dioxide gas bubbles on the shell as it dissolved? Under the shell is a flexible membrane that keeps the egg together.

The Incredible Shrinking Egg

Now you'll take that naked egg and make it shrink and grow again!

Supplies

Naked egg, Corn syrup, Cup, Spoon, Water, Food coloring

*To make a naked egg, try the "Naked Egg" experiment on page 147.

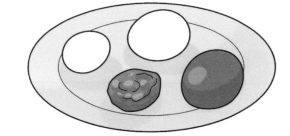

Do It!

1. Put the egg into the cup and pour in enough corn syrup to completely cover the egg.

2. Place a spoon in the cup so it holds the egg down under the corn syrup.

3. Leave the egg in the corn syrup for at least 24 hours.

4. Pull the egg out and rinse it off in water. How has the size of the egg changed?

5. Rinse out the corn syrup from the cup and fill it with water. Add a few drops of food coloring.

6. Put the shrunken egg into the water and leave it for another 24 hours.

7. Pull the egg out of the colored water and rinse it off. How has the size of the egg changed now? What color is the egg?

What's Happening?

The membrane or skin of an egg is semi-permeable. This means that certain molecules, such as oxygen and water, can pass back and forth through the membrane but others, such as corn syrup, cannot.

When you put the egg in the corn syrup, the two liquids try to move so that there are equal amounts or concentrations on both sides of the membrane. However, because the corn syrup can't get into the egg, most of the water moves out of the egg, leaving a shrunken egg behind.

When you put that shrunken egg into a glass of colored water, the water moves back through the membrane and carries the coloring with it. Soon you have a very large egg colored on the inside!

What If?

What if you let the egg sit in other liquids, such as milk and oil? Do these liquids travel through the membrane?

Foldable Egg

Did you ever imagine you could fold up an egg and put it in your pocket? You can with this experiment!

Do It!

1. Use the pushpin to poke a small hole on one end of the egg.

2. Turn the egg over and make a larger hole in the other end of the egg.

3. Now poke several small holes near the larger hole and gently break away the shell between them.

4. Push the bamboo skewer through the larger hole and wiggle it around to scramble the egg in side.

5. Holding the egg over the sink, place the straw over the small hole and blow hard, pushing the egg out of the larger hole and into the sink.

6. Keep blowing until no more egg will come out.

7. Pour a little water into the egg and slosh it around, and then use the straw to blow everything out of the egg again.

8. Place the egg in the cup and pour vinegar into the egg and the cup until the egg is completely covered and stays under the vinegar.

9. Leave the egg for 24 hours.

10. Empty the cup and pour fresh vinegar over the egg. Repeat this process every 24 hours until the shell of the egg is dissolved and you are left with just the membrane.

11. Gently rinse the membrane, inside and out, with water.

12. Carefully squeeze the water out of the membrane, and then blow into one end of the egg to inflate it again. Now you can fold up the egg membrane and then bounce it around in your hand as the air fills up the egg again! You can also sprinkle baby powder on the outside and inside of the egg membrane to keep it from drying out, so it will last

What's Happening?

Unlike the calcium carbonate in the hard eggshell, the egg membrane does not dissolve in vinegar (acetic acid). The membrane is designed to protect the baby chick while it is inside the egg, so it is very flexible and strong. Egg membranes are made of keratin, a protein that makes your own skin strong and flexible, as well!

What If?

What if you use brown or organic eggs? Is there a difference in their membranes or how long it takes for the shell to dissolve?

Egg Strength

Do you think you can crush an egg with just your hand? It might be harder than you think!

Supplies

Raw eggs, Bowl

* Be sure to wash your hands with soap after handling raw eggs to prevent the spread of bacterial diseases like salmonella.

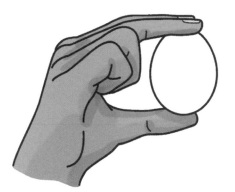

 **Do It!**

1. Take off any rings from your fingers and wrap your whole hand around an egg.

2. Hold the egg over the bowl and squeeze as hard as you can — and then squeeze even harder. Can you break the egg?

3. Hold the egg by its ends, placing your thumb on one end and your index and middle fingers on the other end.

4. Hold the egg over the bowl and squeeze the egg as hard as you can between your fingers. Can you break the egg?

5. Hold the egg in your palm over the bowl, pressing down as hard as you can with just your thumb. Can you break the egg?

What's Happening?

Eggshells alone are very fragile, but the shape of the egg gives it strength. The curved form of the egg spreads the pressure evenly around the egg so even squeezing as hard as you can, you won't break the shell.

The ends of the egg are like arches, making them the strongest parts of the egg. Squeezing the ends of the shell won't break the egg, either. But if you apply a sharp force at a single point, like with your thumb, you will be able to break the eggshell. This is why a hen can sit on the egg without hurting it but the baby chick can peck its way out with a sharp beak.

Balance an Egg

There's a myth that eggs can only be balanced on end during the spring and fall equinoxes because of a stronger gravitational pull from the sun. In fact, an egg can be balanced any day of the year!

Supplies

Raw egg, Flat tabletop, Salt

Do It!

1. Hold the egg so it is standing on end, using just your hands to carefully balance it.
2. If you can't balance it, make a small pile of salt on the table and place the egg on end in the pile of salt. Now can you balance the egg on end?
3. Gently blow the salt out from under the egg to leave the egg standing on end all by itself!

What's Happening?

Throughout the year, weather and day length varies as the Earth's tilt toward the sun changes. However, all year long, the gravitational pull of the sun doesn't change and you are just as likely to balance an egg no matter how many hours of daylight you get.

Walking on Eggshells

Can you literally walk on eggshells without breaking them? Give it a try!

Do It!

Supplies

6 dozen (or more) raw eggs in their cartons, Garbage bag, Friend or a chair

1. Inspect all the eggs and remove any that are cracked.
2. Place all the eggs in the carton, pointy-side down.
3. Lay out the bag and line up the open cartons in two long rows on top of the bag.
4. Place the cartons next to each other with the lids on the outside.
5. Lean on a friend or a chair and gently place your feet on the first two cartons of eggs, keeping your feet completely flat.
6. Walk with flat feet down the eggs to the end. Can you do it without breaking any eggs?

What's Happening?

Eggs are designed to be incredibly strong. The ends of the eggs have an arched shape that allows them to withstand a lot of force. By standing on the eggs with a flat foot, you are probably covering five eggs with each foot. So, if you weigh 100 pounds, each egg only has to support 10 pounds of weight.

Water & Ice

Create your own water park at home with these super cool experiments.

Water Filter

Most of us don't have to worry about finding clean water to drink. We can just turn on the tap or open a bottle. But in some parts of the world, water comes from wells, lakes, and rivers that may not be clean enough to drink. Water filters, like this one, are used to clean the water for drinking.

ADULT NEEDED

DO NOT DRINK the filtered water. This water filter removes visible dirt but not the invisible pathogens that could make you sick.

Supplies

2-liter bottle, Scissors, Coffee filter, Sand, Gravel, Muddy water, Bowl, 3 clear glasses

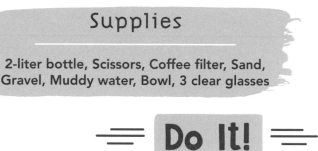

Do It!

1. Ask an adult to help you use the scissors to cut the bottle in half.

2. Take the lid off the bottle, and put the top part upside down, like a funnel, in the bottom part.

3. Put the coffee filter in the bottom of the funnel. (You may need to cut the filter or fold it so that it fits.) You can also wet the filter with clean water so that it sticks to the bottle and stays in place. You want at least one layer of coffee filter covering the opening in the bottom of the funnel.

4. Pour a cup of sand into a bowl of clean water to rinse out any dust.

5. Pour out the clean water and scoop the sand into the funnel so that it sits on top of the coffee filter.

6. Rinse the gravel in the same way and put it on top of the sand.

7. The water filter is now assembled! Pour some of the muddy water into the top of the funnel so that it goes through your filter and drains into the bottom of the bottle.

8. Pour the filtered water into one glass, muddy water into another glass, and clean water from the tap into the last glass. How do the three waters compare? Does the filtered water appear as clear as the tap water?

What's Happening?

As the muddy water flows through your filter, it runs into physical barriers that catch the dirt particles in the water. First the gravel catches the largest pieces of dirt. The sand catches the smaller parts, and the coffee filter catches the tiny bits of dirt you can hardly see.

What If?

What if you add other barriers to your water filter? Try cotton balls, crushed charcoal, and anything else you can think of.

Straw Sprinkler

This simple pump pulls water from a bowl of water and sprays it all around. Make sure to do this experiment outdoors or somewhere you can make a watery mess!

Do It!

Supplies

Straw, Bamboo skewer, Scissors, Tape, Bowl of water

1. Twist and push the pointy end of the skewer through the center of the straw.
2. About an inch on both sides of the skewer, cut part way through the straw so that it can bend open but is still attached.
3. Bend down the two outside pieces of straw to make a triangle with the skewer through the middle.
4. Tape the ends or the straw near the bottom of the skewer to hold them in place. Make sure the bottoms of the straw ends are open.
5. Place the sprinkler into the bowl of water. The bottom of the straw triangle should be in the water but the top should be out of the water.
6. Use your hands to spin the skewer very quickly and watch the water fly!

What's Happening?

When you spin the sprinkler, the water inside the straw spins too. The sides of the spinning straw push the water inwards to make it turn in a circle. Scientists call this centripetal force. Newton's third law of motion says that every force has an equal and opposite re-force, so the water also pushes outward on the straw. Because the straw is sloped, the re-force pushes water up the straw until it flies out the open end at the top.

Ice Cube Rescue

For those times when you need to pull an ice cube out of your drink, but you don't want to get your hands wet and cold!

Do It!

Supplies

Glass of water, Ice cube, Thread, Salt

1. Place the ice cube in the glass of water. Can you use the thread (no hands!) to grab the ice cube and pull it out of the water?
2. Lay the thread on the ice with the ends outside the glass.
3. Sprinkle a little salt on the ice and thread.
4. Wait 15 seconds. Grab the thread and pull out the ice!

What's Happening?

Adding salt to water lowers the temperature at which it melts and freezes. When you put salt on the ice cube, it started to melt, but as the water and ice cooled the melted ice, it froze again—with the thread now inside the ice cube.

Solar Still

If you're ever stranded on a desert island with nothing but salt water to drink, this solar still will come in quite handy!

Supplies

Bowl, Plastic cups 1" shorter than the height of bowl (can be cut to size), Clear plastic wrap, Tape, Small rock, Ruler, Measuring spoon, Measuring cup, Water, Salt

== Do It! ==

1. Pour 2 inches of water into a bowl and mix in 2 tablespoons of salt until it dissolves.
2. Place a plastic cup in the center of the bowl.
3. Stretch plastic wrap over the top of the bowl and seal it with tape.
4. Place small rocks on the center of the plastic wrap above the cup.
5. Press down slightly on the plastic wrap so it stretches and sags down above the cup.
6. You've made a solar still! Place it in bright sunlight.
7. After four hours in the sun, remove the plastic wrap from the bowl and measure the amount of distilled water in the cup. How does the distilled water look and taste?

What's Happening?

The sun heats up the salt water until it evaporates from a liquid to a gas and rises into the air. When the gas hits the cooler plastic wrap, it condenses back into liquid water droplets. Gravity pulls the droplets down the plastic toward the rock, where they drip down into the cup.

Ice Cube Island

You may have seen ice cubes float in a drink, but does cold water float too?

== Do It! ==

Supplies

Water balloons, Bucket, Water

1. Fill a bucket halfway with cold water.
2. Fill a water balloon with cold water.
3. Put the bucket and balloon in the freezer for 10 minutes to get it really cold.
4. Fill the other bucket halfway with hot tap water.
5. Fill a water balloon with hot water too.
6. Put the hot and cold balloon in the bucket of hot water. Do they sink or float?
7. Then put the hot and cold balloon in the bucket of cold water. Do they sink or float?

What's Happening?

Water molecules move around faster in the hot water balloon than in the cold balloon. The hot water has more space between the molecules and is therefore less dense. That's why the hot water balloon floats and the cold water balloon sinks!

Hot + Cold Water

What do you get when you mix hot water with cold? You'll be surprised!

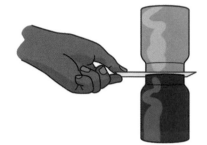

Supplies

2 identical, small glass jars; Red and blue food coloring;
Spoons; Water; Baking pan; 2 index cards
(larger than the tops of your jars)

Do It!

1. Fill one jar to the top with water.
2. Add blue food coloring and stir the water so it is completely blue.
3. Put the jar in the freezer for 10 minutes until it gets very cold, but does not freeze.
4. Fill the other jar to the top with hot water; you can use hot water from the tap or heat the water in the microwave.
5. Add red food coloring and stir the water so it is completely red.
6. Put both jars in the baking pan (to catch any spilled water).
7. Put the index card on top of the blue jar.
8. While holding the index card on top of the jar, quickly and carefully pick up the jar and turn it over. (When the jar is upside down, the card will stay on by itself.)
9. Place the upside-down blue jar on top of the red jar.
10. Look carefully at all sides of the jars to make sure they are lined up exactly on top of each other. Then, carefully pull out the index card. You might want a helper to hold the jars in place while you do this. What happens to the hot red and cold blue water when you remove the index card?
11. Repeat the experiment, but this time, put the cold blue water on the bottom and hot red water on top.

What's Happening?

When you heat water, the molecules move around faster. The quicker hot water molecules are more spread out than the slower-moving cold water molecules. And if the molecules are more spread out, the water is also less dense.

When the denser, cold blue water is on top, it quickly sinks into the less dense, hot red water. The hot red water also rises to the top, causing the two temperatures and colors to mix.

But when the less dense, hot red water is on top, it stays there. The colors don't mix because the less dense liquid is already on top and the denser liquid is on the bottom. If you left the jars until the bottom warmed up and the top cooled down, you would see the colors gradually mix.

Leaky Bottle

How can a water bottle have holes, but no water leaks out?

Supplies

Disposable water bottle full of water,
Tack or safety pin, Sink

Do It!

1. Make sure the bottle is filled completely to the top and the cap is screwed on tightly. Keep the bottle in or next to the sink for the rest of this experiment.

2. Hold the top of the bottle (not the sides) while you use a tack or safety pin to poke a hole in the center of the bottle. Does the water come out?

3. Squeeze the bottle. Does the water come out now?

4. Take the lid off the bottle. What's happening?

5. Refill the bottle and put the cap on tightly.

6. Make two more holes, one near the top of the bottle and another near the bottom.

7. Take off the lid and watch how the water comes out of the three holes.

What's Happening?

The key to this experiment is pressure. The air is pressing in on the outside of the bottle and the water is pressing out on the inside of the bottle.

When you make a hole in the bottle with the cap on, the pressure outside and inside are the same and water does not flow out of the hole.

When you take the cover off the bottle, the pressure inside is greater than the pressure outside because the air is also pushing down on the water and water flows out of the hole.

With three holes in the bottle, you can see the difference in pressure. The water flowing out of the bottom hole goes out much farther than the water flowing out of the top hole. The bottom hole has more pressure because it has more water (and air) above it pushing down. This higher pressure pushes the water out faster!

What If?

What if you trick your friends with this experiment? Start by poking holes all around the bottle. Ask if they want a drink and hand them the bottle while holding it by the cap. When they grab the bottle with their hand, the pressure will cause the bottle to leak all over!

Oil Spill Cleanup

You may have heard of oil accidentally spilling into the ocean. This experiment will give you an idea of how you can clean up spilled oil on a smaller scale.

Supplies

Large baking dish, Water, Vegetable oil, Blue food coloring, Paper towel, Cotton balls, Nylon dish scrubber, Dish soap

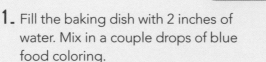

Do It!

1. Fill the baking dish with 2 inches of water. Mix in a couple drops of blue food coloring.
2. Pour 2 tablespoons of oil onto the water to simulate an oil spill in the ocean. Place the paper towel on the oil spill.
3. Wait 30 seconds, and then lift the paper towel. How much of the oil did it soak up?
4. Pour two more oil spills into your blue water and use the cotton balls to clean up one, and the dish scrubber to clean up the other. How much oil did these soak up?
5. Pour one more oil spill into the baking dish ocean.
6. Put 2 drops of dish soap in the middle of the oil and then use your finger to stir the water and oil. What happens to the oil spill?

What's Happening?

The paper towel and cotton balls absorb the oil. You can also add a dispersant like soap or detergent to break up the oil into smaller pieces so that the ocean waves disperse the oil spill. This way it will have a smaller impact on the environment and make it easier for bacteria in the water to break down the oil.

Ketchup Diver

Send a ketchup packet on a deep-sea adventure!

Do It!

Supplies

Empty 2-liter bottle, Ketchup packets, Water, Tall glass

1. Fill the glass almost full of water.
2. Put the ketchup packets in the glass one at a time. Do they float?
3. Find a packet that floats at the top of the glass, but just under the water level. Keep this packet and put away the rest.
4. Remove the label from the 2-liter bottle and fill it with water.
5. Put the ketchup packet in the bottle, fill it all the way to the top with water and put the cap on tightly.
6. Place both hands on the bottle and squeeze. What happens to the ketchup packet in the bottle?

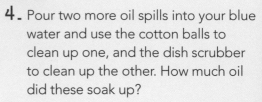

What's Happening?

The ketchup packet floats because it has air inside. When you squeeze the bottle, you also squeeze the ketchup packet and compress the air just enough that it becomes more dense and sinks. When you let go of the bottle, the air expands again, and the ketchup diver returns to the top.

Floating Ball

Will a table tennis ball float in the center of a cup of water?

Do It!

Supplies

Cup, Table tennis ball, Water

1. Fill the cup almost full of water.
2. Put the ball in the water; notice that it floats to the side.
3. Move the ball to the center and let it go. Can you get the ball to stay in the center? Can you get it to stay on the side?
4. Take the ball out and pour more water into the cup to the very top.
5. Put the ball back on the water. Where does it float now? Can you get the ball to stay in the middle? Can you get it to stay on the side?

What's Happening?

Water sticks to itself and forms a skin over the surface. The force that holds the skin together is called surface tension. When the skin touches the edge of the cup, it curves. In a partially full cup, the edge of the water curves up. When you place the ball on the water, it also curves up where it touches the ball and the surface tension pulls on the ball. Unless the ball is exactly in the center of the cup, the ball is pulled by the surface tension to the edge. In an overfull cup of water, the edge curves downward. Now the surface tension pushes on all sides of the ball and keeps it in the center.

Surface Tension Shimmy

Watch water and rubbing alcohol shimmy and shake as their surface tensions battle it out!

Do It!

Supplies

Glass or ceramic plate, 2 cups, Water, Rubbing alcohol, Food coloring, Dropper

1. Pour some water into the cup and mix in a few drops of food coloring.
2. Pour a little of the colored water into the center of the plate so it makes a small puddle of water, about 2 inches across.
3. In another cup, mix some rubbing alcohol with a few drops of a different food coloring.
4. Pour a couple drops of the colored rubbing alcohol into the middle of the colored water puddle. What do you see?

What's Happening?

Water has a much higher surface tension than rubbing alcohol. This means the water sticks to itself much more strongly than it does to the rubbing alcohol. When you drop the rubbing alcohol into the water, the water pulls away, leaving a rubbing alcohol crater. Along the edges, you will see the rubbing alcohol and water shake and shimmy as they eventually mix together.

Water Wheel

Using just the power of water, a water wheel can lift heavy objects!

Supplies

Empty thread spool, Plastic disposable cup, 2-liter bottle, Masking or duct tape, Scissors, Straw, Thread or dental floss, Metal washer

Do It!

1. For the water wheel, cut six identical rectangles from the plastic cup. They should be as long as the spool and about 1 inch wide.
2. Tape the rectangular blades to the spool so they are evenly spaced and curve in the same direction.
3. Put the straw through the hole in the spool.
4. Tape the spool in place in the center of the straw.
5. To make the water wheel holder, ask an adult to help you cut the top off of the 2-liter bottle, and cut two V-shaped notches on opposite sides of the bottle.
6. Poke a couple of holes in the bottom of the bottle for the water to drain out.
7. Cut a piece of thread about 12 inches long and tape one end to the end of the straw.
8. Tie the other end of the string to the metal washer.
9. Put your water wheel holder in the sink, placing the water wheel on the holder so the straw rests in the V-shaped notches and the spool part of the water wheel is right under the faucet.
10. Turn on the water. Does the water wheel spin? If not, adjust the position of the wheel and flow of the water.

What's Happening?

Water wheels are used to lift or turn objects. The motion energy of the falling water is transferred to the wheel, causing it to turn. Anything connected to the wheel will turn, as well.

In this experiment, the straw turns and winds up the string to lift a metal washer. In hydroelectric plants, the wheel turns a giant magnet surrounded by wires. The spinning magnet causes electric current in the wires that can be sent out to power homes with electricity.

What If?

What if you use larger blades? Does it matter how many blades are on the spool? Does the size or number of blades affect how fast your water wheel spins or how much weight it can lift?

Ice Cubes or Oil Cubes?

You know that ice cubes float in water, but what about in oil? And do frozen oil cubes float in oil, or in water?

Supplies

Ice cube tray or 4 small cups, 2 large clear glasses, Vegetable oil, Water, Freezer, Food coloring (optional)

Do It!

1. Fill at least two wells of the ice cube tray all the way to the top with water and at least two with oil.

2. If you like, put a drop or two of different color food coloring in the water ones.

3. Put the tray in the freezer for at least two hours, or until the water and oil cubes are both frozen. Look at the cubes in the ice cube tray. How do the sizes of the ice and oil cubes compare to the size of the water and oil you poured into the tray?

4. Pour water into one glass and oil into the other.

5. Drop one ice cube and one oil cube in each glass. Which cubes float in water and which sink? Which cubes float in oil and which sink?

6. Let the glasses sit out for a couple of minutes until the cubes start to melt. What happens to the water in the oil cup as the ice cube melts? What happens to the oil in the water cup as the oil cube melts?

What's Happening?

Water is the most important liquid on Earth. Humans, plants, and animals could not survive without it. But water is also the most unusual liquid on Earth.

Most liquids, like oil, expand when they are heated, and shrink when they are cooled. You should have noticed that the level of the frozen oil cube was lower than the liquid oil that you poured in the ice tray. The oil shrinks or takes up less space as it freezes. The frozen oil cube also sinks in the liquid oil.

Water is completely different! Like other liquids, water expands when it is heated and shrinks when it is cooled *until* it reaches about 39°F (4°C). Below 39°F, water begins to expand again! Its mass stays the same, but its volume increases. This means that really cold water (below 39°F) and ice float. The frozen ice cube will be larger than the liquid you poured in the ice tray, and the ice cube floats in both the water and the liquid oil.

Super Cool Water

This water is so cool, you can turn it instantly into ice!

Do It!

Supplies

2 unopened bottles of purified water, Ice, Rock salt, Water, Bucket, Thermometer, Bowl, Flavored sugar syrup (optional)

1. Put the bottles in the bucket and cover them with ice.
2. Pour ½ cup of salt over the ice. If you have a large bucket, use more salt.
3. Fill the rest of the bucket with water.
4. Place the thermometer in the bucket, and wait until the temperature reaches 17°F (-8°C).
5. Pull one of the bottles out of the bucket, taking care not to bump the bottle.
6. Hold it by the lid and bang it on the counter. What happens to the water inside the bottle?
7. Place a couple of ice cubes in the bowl.
8. Carefully pull the other bottle out of the bucket.
9. Unscrew the top and slowly pour the water onto the ice cubes. What happens to the water as you pour? If you have flavored sugar syrup or juice, pour it in the bowl for an instant snow cone!

What's Happening?

Water freezes at 0°C or 32°F, but it needs to be a crystal or seed to start the process. In water from your tap, there are minerals and other chemicals in the water that make this happen. Because purified water is "pure," it can be cooled below freezing or super cooled without forming ice. Once the water is super cooled, a small bubble or piece of ice can start the freezing process.

Ice Cube on a Wire

An ice cube on a wire would make a very COOL necklace on a hot day!

Do It!

Supplies

18-inch piece of thin wire, 2 pencils, Sturdy plastic cup, Ice cube

1. Wrap each end of the wire around a pencil several times, until you have about 8 inches of wire stretched between the pencils.
2. Turn the cup upside down and place the ice cube on top.
3. Hold the pencils like handles and place the top of the wire across the toothpick.
4. Pull down hard on the pencils for a few minutes. What happens to the wire?
5. Stop pulling when the wire is all the way inside the ice cube. You have an ice cube on a wire!

What's Happening?

Pressure melts ice. Scientists call this regelation. For instance, the pressure from an ice skate melts the top layer of ice, so a skater glides on a thin layer of water. When the pressure is removed, the water refreezes. It appears as if the wire was frozen in the ice cube!

Walking Water

Watch water defy gravity!

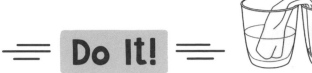

= Do It! =

Supplies

Paper towel, Scissors, 3 clear glasses, Water, Food coloring

1. Cut the paper towel in half lengthways, and then fold it in half lengthways twice, so you have a long strip that is four layers thick.
2. Pour water into two of the glasses so they are almost full.
3. Put two colors of food coloring in each glass.
4. Place the three glasses in a row with the empty glass in the middle.
5. Put one end of a strip in the empty glass, and the other in one of the glasses of colored water.
6. Do the same with the other strip, but put one end in the other glass of colored water.
7. If the middle of the strips stick up in the air, slide the glasses apart a bit so they stay flat on top.
8. Wait 15 minutes, and then check on the glasses. What do you see?
9. Check again after 30 minutes. Has anything changed?

What's Happening?

The water moves along the paper towel using capillary action. The water sticks to itself (called cohesion) but it sticks to the paper towel (called adhesion) more. The water crawls up the tiny gaps in the fibers of the paper towel. This is the same method plants use to get water from their roots to the tips of their leaves.

Soap-powered Boat

Sail the soapy seas with this simple ship!

= Do It! =

Supplies

Foam egg carton, Scissors, Bowl of water, Dish soap, Toothpick

1. Cut out a boat from the flat top of the egg carton, about 2 inches long and 1 inch wide.
2. Cut a point at the top of the boat so it's shaped like a house.
3. Cut a small, upside-down-triangle-shaped hole from the bottom of the boat.
4. Place your boat in the center of the water.
5. Dip the tip of the toothpick into the dish soap and then dip it into the hole at the bottom of the boat. Watch your boat zoom around!

What's Happening?

The water in the bowl sticks together, especially on the top of the water. This stickiness is called surface tension and forms a skin on top of the water that is hard to break. This is one reason your boat floats on top of the water instead of sinking to the bottom. The soap has a much smaller surface tension. The surface tension skin on top of the water pulls away from the soap like a balloon popping. This sends your boat zooming.

Soft Water, Hard Water

Most water contains tiny amounts of minerals that give it a unique taste and affects how it makes bubbles.

Supplies

3 different sources of water, 3 clear 20-oz. soda bottles, Ruler, Ivory dish soap, Measuring cup, Stopwatch or clock

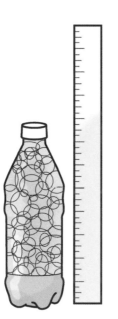

Do It!

Before you begin, find water from at least three different places where you want to measure the water hardness. For example, the faucet at your house, bottled water from the store, your best friend's house, your school, or the water fountain at the playground. The farther away these places are from each other, the better.

1. Use the measuring cup to pour exactly 1 cup of water into a soda bottle for each place from which you are collecting water.

2. Label the bottles.

3. Place two drops of soap into the first bottle and screw the top on very tight.

4. Shake the bottle as hard as you can for a full 60 seconds.

5. As soon as you are done shaking the bottle, use the ruler to measure the total height of the bubbles in the bottle. If the water is very soft, the whole bottle may be filled with bubbles. If the water is very hard, you may not have any bubbles at all! Most places will be somewhere in between.

6. Repeat the process for the other bottles of water. How does the amount of bubbles from each place compare?

What's Happening?

Water hardness is a measure of the minerals in water. Hard water has more minerals than soft water. If you live near an ocean, you probably have soft water because removing salt from water also takes out the minerals that make water hard.

If you get your water from a river, your water is probably hard. The flowing water from rivers takes minerals out of the rocks in the riverbeds. Well water is usually hard too. Wells pull up water that is in between layers of rock underground. This water dissolves minerals from the rocks.

Hero's Engine

Hero was a Greek engineer who lived in Alexandria about 2,000 years ago. He invented the first steam engine using the same science as the engine you can make here with a cup, straws, and water!

Supplies

Large foam cup, Pen or sharp pencil, String, Scissors, 2 bendy straws, Water, Sink or large bowl

Do It!

1. Use the pen to poke two small holes near the top of the cup on opposite sides.

2. Thread a piece of string through the holes and tie a knot a couple of inches above the top of the cup so that there is extra string above the knot.

3. Cut both straws so there is about 1 inch of straight straw on either side of the bendy parts.

4. Use the pen again to poke two slightly larger holes about ½ inch from the bottom on opposite sides of the cup. The holes should be just large enough for the straws to fit snuggly.

5. Slide a straw into each hole so that the bendy part is on the outside of the cup.

6. Straighten the straws so they both stick directly out from the cup.

7. Hold the cup by the extra string over the sink or a large bowl and pour water into the cup. Does water come out of the straws? Does the cup move?

8. Bend the straws so they both point clockwise.

9. Fill the cup with water and hold it over the sink again. Does water come out of the straws? Does the cup move now?

What's Happening?

Air pressure pushes the water out of the cup and through the bent straws. But Newton's third law tells us that every force has an equal and opposite re-force.

This means the water also pushes back on the straws, causing the cup to spin around. The cup spins in the opposite direction that the water moves and with the same force that pushes the water out of the straws.

In Hero's original steam engine, called an *aeolipile*, the curved straws would be at the top of a sealed metal cup. Fire is used to heat the water in the cup and it turns to steam. As the steam rushes out of the straws, the cup turns. This turning motion could be used to pull a rope and move heavy objects or turn wheels to grind up grain.

Moving Molecules

What makes hot water hot and cold water cold?

Supplies

3 clear jars, Water, Food coloring

Do It!

1. Fill one jar with water and leave it on the counter for 30 minutes.
2. Fill another jar and put it in the freezer for 10 minutes to get very cold but not freeze.
3. Fill the third jar with hot tap water. You may need to work on the timing so that you have a jar of room temperature water, a jar of cold water, and a jar of hot water at the same time.
4. Add three drops of food coloring to each jar. What happens to the food coloring in the different temperatures?

What's Happening?

Heating water adds energy. This energy causes the water molecules to move around faster. Cooling water removes energy and the water molecules slow down. When you add food coloring to the jars with different temperatures of water, you can see the water molecules moving!

In the jar of hot water, the fast-moving molecules mix the color into the water. In the jar of cold water, the color sinks to the bottom of the slow-moving water. The water at room temperature is somewhere in between.

Pepper Scatter

This experiment is so simple and dramatic, you might even think it's magic!

Supplies

Bowl, Water, Ground pepper, Liquid soap

Do It!

1. Fill the bowl with water. Sprinkle pepper over the water.
2. Stick your finger in the middle of the bowl. What's happening?
3. Put a tiny amount of liquid soap on the tip of your finger. Stick your finger in the middle of the bowl again. What happens now?

What's Happening?

First, pepper is hydrophobic. This means it is not attracted to water. This helps to keep it dry and on top of the water.

Second, water is attracted to itself and sticks together. This causes a skin of water on the surface that is hard to break called surface tension. The pepper sits on top of the surface tension skin. When you add soap to the water, the skin breaks. The soap gets between the water molecules so they can't stick together. The skin pops like a balloon when you touch it with soap and carries the pepper out to the edge of the bowl.

Bottle Pour

What's the quickest way to empty water from a bottle?

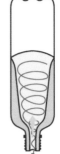

═ Do It! ═

Supplies

3 identical bottles of water, Stopwatch, Friend, Sink

1. Have your friend time how long it takes to pour the water from a bottle into the sink using each of these methods.

Method 1: Turn the bottle completely upside down.

Method 2: Turn the bottle sideways, at an angle, so the water comes out smoothly.

Method 3: Turn the bottle completely upside down and swirl it continuously so the water moves around the inside of the bottle like a tornado. Which method emptied the bottle quickest?

What's Happening?

With each method, gravity pulls the water out of the bottles. However, to get water out of a bottle, air needs to get in to fill up the empty space where the water used to be.

When you held the bottle upside down, air bubbles went up through the bottle. This is not the quickest way to let water out and air in. When you turn the bottle sideways, there is plenty of room for the air to come in, but the water comes out slowly because the bottle is sideways. When you hold the bottle upside down and swirl it, you provide a hole in the middle for air to come in as gravity pulls the water out of the bottle.

Penny Drop

How many drops of water fit on top of a penny? You might be surprised!

═ Do It! ═

Supplies

Clean penny, Dropper, Water, Rubbing alcohol, Vegetable oil, Dish soap, Paper towel

1. Lay a paper towel on a flat surface and place the penny in the middle.
2. Fill the dropper with water. Hold the dropper close to the penny and place a drop of water on it.
3. Slowly add drops until the penny overflows and spills onto the paper towel.
4. Repeat with alcohol, oil, and dish soap, making sure you clean the penny before adding drops of liquid. How many drops of each liquid can you fit on the penny?

What's Happening?

Most liquids stick to each other. This stickiness forms a skin over the surface of the liquid. The skin holds a drop together, which is why a drop appears rounded. The force that holds this skin together is called surface tension. Liquids with the strongest surface tension skins, such as water, can fit the most drops on the coin. Eventually, you will add so much liquid that the skin can't hold it all in and it pops.

In the Bathroom

You'll look at your restroom differently after trying these awe-inspiring experiments.

Down the Drain

Do toilets flush one way in the Southern Hemisphere and another way in the Northern Hemisphere?

Supplies

Sinks, Toilets

═ Do It! ═

Sink Test

1. Fill the sink halfway with water, and then turn the water off. Wait at least three minutes until the water is completely still. Make sure no one walks near the sink or disturbs the water in any way. You want to be sure that no other factors affect the direction in which the water drains.

2. Slowly and carefully remove the plug and watch the water drain down the sink.

3. Write down the direction in which the water spins. Does the direction change while the water drains?

4. Test each sink at least three times.

Toilet Test

5. Find a clean toilet and, just like with the sink, make sure the water is very still.

6. Flush the toilet. Write down the direction in which the water spins. Does the water pouring back into the toilet affect the direction in which the water drains?

7. Test the same toilet at least three more times. Test as many sinks and toilets as you can. Did the water always drain the same way? What factors do you think might affect the direction in which water drains?

What's Happening?

The Coriolis force is caused by the rotation of the Earth. Everything on the planet rotates with the Earth. If you could look down on the North Pole of the spinning Earth, you would see that it turns counterclockwise. If you then look at the South Pole, you would see it spins clockwise. Check this out on a globe!

But because the Earth rotates relatively slowly — about once every day — this force is extremely small. For large amounts of slow-moving fluids, such as the atmosphere, it has a larger, lasting effect. Hurricanes in the Northern Hemisphere spin counterclockwise, and in the Southern Hemisphere they spin clockwise — just like the Earth. Also like the Earth, hurricanes turn relatively slowly and the direction of the spin is controlled by the direction in which the Earth spins.

For smaller amounts of a fluid, such as the water in your toilet, this force is easily overcome by even the tiniest disturbances and design flaws in the sink. These factors are more likely than the Coriolis force to influence the direction in which the water drains.

Plunger Power

A plunger is a useful tool when the toilet backs up – and to demonstrate of the power of air pressure!

Supplies

Toilet plunger, Petroleum jelly, Hardcover books, Rubber bands

== Do It! ==

1. Rub petroleum jelly along the outer edge of the plunger.
2. Hold one of the books closed with rubber bands.
3. Lay the book on the floor and push the plunger forcefully onto the book (not the rubber bands), so that it squishes and pushes the air out. Lift the plunger straight up. Can you lift the book?
4. Attach more books with rubber bands. How many books can you lift?

What's Happening?

Plungers get their power from air pressure. When you squish a plunger on a flat surface and push the air out, you are creating a vacuum. That means there is very little air inside the plunger. However, outside of the plunger, there is a lot of air pushing very hard. Almost 15 pounds of force pushes on every square inch from the weight of the air! This is the force that holds the books onto the plunger.

Oil + Water = ?

Oil and water don't mix…or do they?

Supplies

Clear cup, Water, Vegetable oil, Bar of soap, 3 toothpicks

== Do It! ==

1. Fill the cup half full of water. Use a toothpick to place a few drops of oil into the water.
2. Use a clean toothpick to try to break up the oil drops. What happens?
3. Rub the third toothpick on the bar of soap and try to break up the oil drops. What happens now?

What's Happening?

Oil and water don't mix. Water molecules stick to each other stronger than they stick to oil. Because oil molecules are not packed together as tightly as water molecules, oil is less dense and floats on top of water.

However, when you add soap, something changes. Soap molecules, or surfactants, have two ends: one that is attracted to water and another that is attracted to oil. The soap surrounds the oil molecules with the end that is attracted to oil so that they can break up and move around the water. There is even a special word for an oil molecule surrounded by soap: micelle. By adding soap to the oil, you create tiny micelles on top of the water!

Mirror, Mirror in the Steam

Have you ever stepped out of a hot shower and saw a steamed-up mirror? Why does that happen?

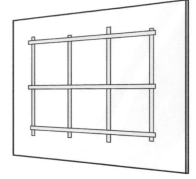

Supplies

Large mirror, Shower (in the same room as the mirror), Shaving cream, Bar of soap, Liquid hand soap, Dishwashing soap, Potato, Paper towels, Glass cleaner, Masking tape, Pen

Do It!

1. Clean the mirror well with glass cleaner. Use the masking tape to divide your mirror into six 6-inch squares.

2. On the tape, label the squares with the name of each item you will be testing, leaving one square blank. You will compare the other squares to this one and use it to make sure the mirror really fogs up.

3. Cut the potato in half and rub the inside of the potato over the square labeled "Potato." Use a dry paper towel to rub the mirror until it is shiny again.

4. In the square labeled "Bar of Soap," rub the dry bar of soap over the mirror in the square. Then use a dry paper towel to rub the mirror until it's shiny again.

5. Do the same thing in the other squares with the liquid hand soap, shaving cream, and dishwashing soap.

6. Now it's time to get clean! Take a long, hot shower. Which squares got steamy and which stayed steam-free? Leave the squares on the mirror for a week and look every time someone in the house takes a shower to see which squares stayed steam-free.

What's Happening?

When you take a hot shower, you might notice clouds of steam in the air. The water is so hot that it changes from water (a liquid) to steam (a gas). This is called evaporation. When this steam hits your cold mirror, it turns back into water and sticks to the mirror. This is called condensation. If you look close at the steamed-up mirror, you will see tiny drops of water all over the mirror.

One way to keep your mirror from steaming is to warm up the mirror so the steam doesn't condense back to water. Or you can put something on the mirror so that the water doesn't bead up into tiny drops when it condenses. Certain chemicals, such as glycerin, mix well with water and are called hydrophilic. This causes the water to spread out over the mirror so that you can see yourself.

Floating Bowling Balls

Can you float a bowling ball in the bathtub?
The results are striking!

Supplies

Bathtub, Bowling ball (12 pounds or less), Bowling ball (heavier than 12 pounds), 6 cups of salt

═ Do It! ═

1. Fill your bathtub almost full of water, leaving a few inches at the top.
2. Gently place the bowling balls in the bathtub. What happens?
3. Pour salt into the tub and mix it around. Does anything change?

What's Happening?

All bowling balls, no matter their weight, are the same size or volume, with a circumference of 27 inches. Because they have the same volume, this means that heavier bowling balls are denser, while lighter bowling balls are less dense. When you put the bowling balls in the tub, the ball that is 12 pounds or less floats! Anything heavier than 12 pounds will sink to the bottom. When you add salt to the water, you make it denser, so that even a 16-pound bowling ball will float. You should have seen both bowling balls in the tub float after you added the salt.

Soap Clouds

ADULT NEEDED

What happens when you microwave soap?

Supplies

4 bars of soap, including Ivory, Bowl of water; Microwave oven; 4 paper plates

═ Do It! ═

1. Place the bars in a bowl of water. Which soaps float? Which sink? Remove the bars and dry them off.
2. Place each soap on its own plate and put one plate of soap in the microwave. Cook the soap on high for one minute.
3. Remove the soap and wait two minutes for it to cool. How is it different from before it was cooked? Does it look or feel different?
4. Cook each of the soaps, one at a time, for one minute in the microwave and observe any changes.

What's Happening?

Ivory soap is the only soap that floats. Look carefully at it, and you'll notice tiny bubbles all over its surface. This is because Ivory soap has air bubbles whipped into it, unlike other soaps. When you cook Ivory soap in the microwave, the soap becomes soft and the air and moisture trapped in those bubbles heats up and expands, making a foam. The other bars of soap melt.

Oily Water Mix-up

Water and oil don't mix - unless they get a little help!

Supplies

Clean bottle with a lid, Water, Vegetable oil, Shampoo, Measuring cup

═ Do It! ═

1. Pour ½ cup of water into the jar. Pour ¼ cup of vegetable oil down the inside of the jar.
2. Cover the jar and shake it hard for 30 seconds. Do the liquids look mixed together? Let the jar sit for five minutes. The water and oil should separate into two layers.
3. Squeeze some shampoo into the jar and watch what happens.
4. Cover the jar and shake it hard for 30 seconds. Are the oil and water mixed up? Let the jar sit for five minutes. Do the water and oil separate into two layers?

What's Happening?

Oil and water don't mix because they stick to themselves and not to each other. Soap, on the other hand, sticks to just about everything. Scientists call soap a surfactant. These stick to the oil and water, allowing the oil and water to stick to each other. With soap around, oil and water DO mix!

Toilet Paper Inertia

What's the most efficient way to remove toilet paper from the roll?

Supplies

Full roll of toilet paper hanging on a holder

═ Do It! ═

1. Unroll the toilet paper on the holder. Can you get enough paper on the floor so that it rolls on its own?
2. Roll the paper back up. Hold the end of the paper (near the roll) with both hands and yank it. The paper should rip right off.

What's Happening?

The key to controlling how the toilet paper rolls is inertia. The concept comes from Newton's first law: "An object at rest remains at rest and an object in motion remains in motion unless acted on by a force." Inertia is this tendency to remain at rest or motion and depends on the mass of the object. In our case, the object is a roll of toilet paper. In the first part of the experiment, your force was just large enough to get the paper rolling and keep it rolling. But in the second part, the inertia of the "massive" paper roll kept it at rest while the less massive piece ripped off.

Wrinkly Fingers

Have you ever taken a bath or spent hours in the pool and then your fingers and toes are all wrinkly? For a long time, people thought that skin absorbing water caused the wrinkles. But if that's the case, why doesn't your whole body get wrinkly?

Supplies

3 large bowls, 10 marbles, 5 or more volunteers, Stopwatch

Do It!

1. Fill one large bowl with warm water. Have a volunteer hold both hands in the water for 20 to 30 minutes, until their fingertips are completely wrinkly.

2. Place 10 marbles in one of the bowls, and then place the bowl of marbles on one side of your volunteer and an empty bowl on the other side.

3. Ask the volunteer to move the dry marbles, one at a time, from one bowl to the other, transferring each marble from one hand to another on the way. Time how long it takes them to move all the marbles.

4. Pour water into the bowl with the marbles and have your volunteer soak their hands for a few more minutes to keep them wrinkly.

5. Again, time how long it takes your volunteer to move the wet marbles from one bowl to the other in the same way.

6. Let your volunteer take a break so their fingers dry out and become un-wrinkly again.

7. Repeat the experiment with smooth fingertips, and wet and dry marbles.

8. Use several volunteers (at least five) to do the same experiment, mixing up whether they start with wet or dry hands. Average the times for each of the four situations. Under which conditions did your volunteers move the marbles the quickest?

What's Happening?

Since the 1930s, scientists knew that finger wrinkling was controlled by your body's autonomic nervous system, the system that also controls your breathing, heart rate, and perspiration. They noticed that people with nerve damage do not get wrinkly fingers in the water and realized that finger wrinkling is caused by blood vessels constricting below the skin.

One theory about the reason our fingers wrinkle when they get wet is that, like the treads on a tire, the wrinkles increase your grip on wet objects. Scientists have performed experiments like this one and gotten mixed results as to whether wrinkled fingers really do make it easier to hold on to wet objects. What do you think?

Elephant Toothpaste

This foam explosion creates what looks like toothpaste that's big enough for an elephant!

Supplies

20-oz. soda bottle, Funnel, Hydrogen peroxide, Dish soap, Yeast, Small bowl, Measuring spoon, Measuring cup, Safety glasses and clothes, Plastic wash basin

Do It!

1. In the small bowl, mix 2 teaspoons of yeast in 2 tablespoons of warm water.
2. Funnel ½ cup of hydrogen peroxide into the bottle. Add three drops of dish soap and swish the bottle around to mix.
3. Place the bottle in the basin. Pour the yeast solution into the bottle, quickly remove the funnel, and get out of the way!

What's Happening?

Hydrogen peroxide is water with an extra oxygen atom — H_2O_2. It's not very stable, and slowly decomposes into water and oxygen. The yeast speeds up, or catalyzes, the process so that all the oxygen gas is released quickly. The gas gets trapped in the soap, creating LOTS of bubbles, resembling toothpaste for an elephant. When the experiment is over, you're left with water, soap, and a little yeast.

Bubble Snakes

Why bother with one bubble when you can have a giant snake of bubbles?

Supplies

6-inch square of the following fabrics: Cotton, Jersey, Terry cloth, and Nylon; Empty 16-oz. soda bottle; Scissors; Rubber band; Bowl; Liquid dish soap; Outdoor space

Do It!

1. Cut the bottom off the bottle. Stretch one piece of fabric over the large end. Secure it with a rubber band.
2. Mix 1 cup of water and ¼ cup of liquid soap in the bowl.
3. Put the cloth end of the bottle into the bowl so the fabric soaks up the soap.
4. Take the bottle out and blow into the small end of the bottle as hard as you can. A snake of bubbles should grow out of the fabric.
5. Repeat the process with the other fabrics. Which fabric made the longest snake? Which fabric was easiest to blow through?

What's Happening?

When you blow through your bubble snake maker, you are creating hundreds of tiny bubbles that stick together. The number and size of the bubbles depend on the holes in the fabric. Bigger holes mean bigger bubbles!

Bomb Your Bath

These bath bombs combine the fun of bubbles with soothing bath salts.

ADULT NEEDED

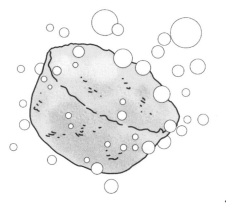

Supplies

Mini muffin pan, Large bowl, Small bowl, Masking tape, Marker, Water, Vegetable oil, Citric acid, Baking soda, Cornstarch, Epsom salt, Dropper, Measuring spoon, Spoons for mixing, Thermometer, Stopwatch, Oven

Do It!

1. In the large bowl, mix together 2 tablespoons of citric acid, 4 tablespoons of baking soda, 3 tablespoons of cornstarch and 1 tablespoon of Epsom salt.

2. In the small bowl, mix together 2 teaspoons of water and 2 teaspoons of vegetable oil.

The next few steps are tricky, so read ahead to be ready!

3. Have a clean spoon ready. Add two drops of the oil mixture to the dry mixture. Use the back of the spoon to pat down the fizzing, mixing in the damp part with the dry mixture.

4. Repeat this until all the oil mixture has been added to the dry mixture. It should be damp enough to hold its shape.

5. Place a drop of vegetable oil in each muffin tray well. Spread the oil over each well with your finger. Spoon the mixture into the pan and push down to pack the mixture tight.

6. Preheat the oven to 170°F. Place the pan in the oven, and then turn the oven off. Leave the pan in the oven with the door closed for one hour. While the bath bombs are drying, clean out the big bowl.

7. Remove the bath bombs from the tray. If they are crumbly, try again with more liquid.

8. Fill the large bowl with hot water. Drop the bath bomb in the water and time how long it takes to stop fizzing.

What's Happening?

The fizz of the bath bomb comes from the citric acid and baking soda. Baking soda is a base and citric acid is — surprise! — an acid. When you mix these together, they produce a salt and carbon dioxide gas. This gas is what makes that fun fizz.

The longevity of the fizz depends on the amount of baking soda and citric acid in the bath bomb AND how easily they can get together. If there is a lot of cornstarch, it takes longer to dissolve, and you get a longer fizz time. This also means you will have a less impressive fizz, because it's spread out over a longer time.

Light & Color

Create your own indoor rainbow and other incredible creations using the properties of light.

Break a Pencil

Use the power of light and water to break a pencil into two pieces.

Supplies

Tall, clear glass of water; Pencil

Do It!

1. Hold the pencil straight up and down in the center of the glass of water. What do you see? Slowly move the pencil all the way to one side of the glass. What happens to the pencil in the water?

What's Happening?

Light travels faster in air than in water. Add that to the round shape of the glass, and you have an interesting result. When the pencil is right in the middle of the glass, the light travels straight from the pencil to your eyes without bending. The light hits the front of the glass straight on as it travels from the pencil through the water into the air to your eyes. You might notice that the pencil looks a little fatter in the water. The curve of the glass acts as a magnifying glass.

As you move the pencil to the side of the glass, the light from the pencil no longer goes straight to your eyes, but instead comes in at an angle. When the light passes through the water and comes out into the air, the light speeds up. But not all the light from the pencil speeds up at the same time. Because the light is coming out at an angle, some of the light will come out into the air first and the rest just after. This causes the light rays to bend, and the part of the pencil underwater appears closer to the side of the glass than the part of the pencil above the water. In fact, if you move the pencil all the way to the side of the glass, the part underwater disappears completely. The light is bent so much that it doesn't even get to your eyes.

What If?

What if you try other liquids, such as corn syrup or mineral oil? How does dissolving salt or sugar in the water change how the light is bent?

Color Explosion

Watch colors dance in milk.

Do It!

Supplies

Plate, Whole milk, Food coloring, Cotton swab, Dish soap

1. Fill the plate with milk.
2. Place two drops of each color in the center of the plate.
3. Dip the cotton swab in soap. Touch the swab to the center of the colors. Watch the colors explode! Touch the swab to the milk in other places on the plate to keep the colors moving.

What's Happening?

Milk is mostly water. Water molecules have positive and negative ends that stick to each other, creating a skin on the surface of the milk. Fats and proteins are mixed in with the water and interact differently with the soap. Soap has a negative end that latches onto the positive end of the water. This prevents the water from sticking to itself, and the skin rushes off the surface of the milk, carrying the colors with it. As the soap interacts with the fats and proteins, the water and colors swirl around.

Candy Chromatography

What dyes are in your candies?

Do It!

Supplies

Candy-coated chocolate pieces (such as M&Ms), Paper towel, Scissors, Pencil, Plate, Tall jar, Water, Salt, Clear tape

1. Cut the paper towel into strips 1 inch taller than the jar and 1 inch wide. Label the top of each strip with each candy's color. Draw a line 1 inch from the bottom of each strip.
2. Pour 1 inch of water into the jar. Add a pinch of salt.
3. Place each colored candy on the plate. Put a drop of water next to each, and then place the candy on the drop. Let the candies sit for three minutes, and then remove them. Place the matching filter strip on the colored drop above the line. Let it soak up the color.
4. Place the strips into the jar with the bottom, not the color, touching the water. Tape them in place.
5. Leave the strips in the jar until the water is 2 inches from the top. Let the strips dry. How many colors do you see?

What's Happening?

The water moves up the strips using capillary action. The water sticks to the paper towel more than it sticks to itself and moves up the strip. The dyes in the candies move with the water, but some colors move faster than others, so they separate on the filter.

Color-mixing Spinner

Mixing colors of light is very different from mixing colors of paint or ink.

Supplies

Cereal box,
White paper,
Cup, Scissors,
Glue, Markers,
String

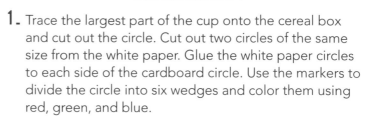

Do It!

1. Trace the largest part of the cup onto the cereal box and cut out the circle. Cut out two circles of the same size from the white paper. Glue the white paper circles to each side of the cardboard circle. Use the markers to divide the circle into six wedges and color them using red, green, and blue.

2. Use the scissors to poke two holes about an inch apart on either side of the center of the circle. Cut a piece of string about 3 feet long. Thread the string through the two holes in the circle and tie the ends together.

3. Slide the circle to the middle of the string and hold one end of the string in each hand. Twirl the circle around so the string gets all twisted around. Then pull outward on the strings to watch the circle spin. What color do you see when the red, blue, and green colors mix? On a piece of scrap paper, mix red, blue, and green inks using the markers. How do these two colors compare?

4. Make color-mixing spinners with just red and green, red and blue, or blue and green. What colors do you see when they mix on the spinner?

What's Happening?

The spinning motion of the cardboard circle mixes the colored light you see reflected off the spinner. The primary colors of light are red, blue, and green. When you mix together these colors in light, you get white. The primary colors of paint or ink are yellow, cyan, and magenta. When you mix together these colors in paint or ink, you get black. Inks and light colors mix differently. Red and green light makes yellow, blue and green light makes cyan, and red and blue light makes magenta.

What If?

What if you color your color-mixing spinner with yellow, cyan, and magenta? What other color combinations can you try?

Crookes Radiometer

When William Crookes first built his radiometer in 1873, he thought that the black and white flags spun around because light pushes on shiny surfaces. It turns out he was wrong. Can you figure out what really happens?

Supplies

Clear jar with lid, Aluminum foil, Scissors, Ruler, Black paint, Glue stick, Thread, Toothpick, Tape, Black paper, Bright sun or lamp with incandescent bulb

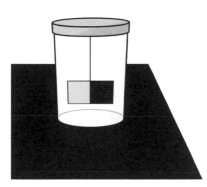

═ ▶ Do It! ═

1. Cut out two 1-inch square pieces of foil. Paint one side of each piece black.

2. Cut a piece of thread a few inches longer than the height of the jar. Tie one end to the center of the toothpick. Use the glue stick to attach the foil pieces to the toothpick so that they hang down like flags. The foil pieces should face in opposite directions so each side of the toothpick has a black and shiny foil flag.

3. Tape the other end of the thread to the inside lid of the jar. Adjust the length of the thread so that the toothpick flags hang about 1 inch from the bottom of the jar and don't touch the sides. Make sure the foil is completely flat before putting the lid on the jar.

4. Lay out some black paper in a bright, sunny spot outside or near a lamp with an incandescent bulb. Leave the jar on the black paper in the bright light. It will take several seconds for the toothpick to stop moving. As the light hits the paper, it will start to slowly turn around.

What's Happening?

Radiometer is a misleading name for this experiment. The spinning of the flags is not caused by the brightness of the light, but rather by the heat absorbed by the black flag compared to the white or shiny flag. The air molecules inside the jar flow between the warmer black flag and the cooler white flag, causing them to spin around. By placing the radiometer on black paper, the radiometer can heat up quicker to help it spin faster. Radiometers purchased at stores have a partial vacuum. That means most (but not all) of the air has been pulled out of the jar. Enough air remains inside to keep the flags spinning but not to slow them down. The radiometer you make will move slower because there is more air resistance in the jar.

Disappearing Bowl

How do you see things that are clear?

Supplies

Large glass bowl, Smaller glass bowl made of Pyrex, Vegetable oil

Do It!

1. Fill the large bowl ⅓ full of oil. Place the smaller bowl in the large bowl. Add oil until the level of the oil is almost level with the top of the small bowl. Can you see the large bowl? Can you see the smaller bowl? Pour oil into the smaller bowl. Can you see the small bowl now?

What's Happening?

Clear objects are visible because we can see the light bounce off (reflect) or bend through (refract). Light bends because it slows when it moves from the air to the glass, and then speeds up again when it moves out of the glass into the air. In this experiment, the speed of light in oil is the same as the speed of light in Pyrex glass. When the empty bowl is sitting in oil, you can see the bowl because the light bends when it enters the air inside the bowl. When you fill the bowl with oil, it disappears because the light does not bend as it moves from the oil to the Pyrex glass and back to the oil again.

Disappearing Coin

Make your money disappear by spending it, or use science!

Supplies

2 clear cups, 2 coins, Water, Table, Straw

Do It!

1. Sit at a table and place the cups a foot from the edge. Place a coin inside one cup and a coin underneath the other cup. Can you see both coins?
2. Fill both cups with water. Can you see the coins now? Use the straw to place two drops of water on the coin underneath the cup. Can you see the coin?

What's Happening?

Light bends when it hits a clear object because the speed of light is different inside the clear object than it is in the air. When light hits the empty clear cup, it bends and you can see the coin in and under the cup. When you fill both cups with water, the light travels through the water and to your eye. The air between the cup and the coin causes the light to bend just enough so that you can't see the coin under the cup when the cups are away from you. If you look down into the cup, you will see the coin underneath.

Reappearing Coin

First you don't see it ... and then you do!

Supplies

Paper cup,
Coin, Water

Do It!

1. Place a coin in the empty cup. Look down in the cup to see the coin, and then move your head back until it is just out of view. Keep your head in place while you pour water into the cup. Can you see the coin now?

What's Happening?

When you view the coin in the cup, light reflects straight off the coin to your eye. When you move your head, the side of the cup gets in the way so the light reflected off the coin doesn't make it to your eye. However, when you pour water into the cup, the light reflected off the coin travels through the water and into the air. It then bends upward, as the speed of light is faster in air. This bending allows the light from your coin to reach your eye. What was hidden by the cup is now revealed!

Indoor Rainbow

The best part of a rainstorm is the rainbow afterward. Now you can make your own rainbow indoors whenever you want.

Supplies

Bowl, Water,
Mirror,
Flashlight,
White paper

Do It!

1. Fill the bowl most of the way with water. Put the mirror in the bowl so that it leans against the side of the bowl at an angle and is at least halfway under the water.

2. Hold the paper above the bowl with one hand. Use the other hand to shine the flashlight onto the part of the mirror that is under the water. What do you see on the paper?

What's Happening?

The white light from a flashlight is made up of all the colors of the rainbow. When that light hits the water, it slows down. Because the flashlight is shining on the water at an angle, and not straight on, the light bends when it slows down. The different colors of the light bend different amounts, so they are spread out into a rainbow of colors. The mirror in the water reflects the rainbow up onto the paper so that you can see it.

Measure the Speed of Light

Light is incredibly fast. It travels at about 300 million meters every second! How can you measure something so fast? With the light-creating box in your kitchen—also known as a microwave oven.

Supplies

Microwave oven, Large chocolate bar, Ruler, Calculator

Do It!

1. Take out the wheels inside your microwave that make your food spin around while it's cooking. We want the plate to stay still for this experiment.

2. Place the chocolate upside down on the plate so there is a long, smooth chocolate surface. Put the plate in the microwave and heat it on high for 15 seconds.

3. Remove the plate and look for the melted spots on the chocolate. Use the ruler to measure the distance between the close edges of two melted spots in centimeters. These two spots are where the light wave went into the chocolate bar and came back out again, and is equal to half of a wavelength. Use your calculator to divide that distance by 100. This is the distance in meters. Multiply that number by 2 to get the full wavelength in meters.

4. Look on the door or back of your microwave to find the frequency of the light waves it uses to cook your food. Most microwaves have a frequency of 2450 MHz, which is 2,450,000,000 waves per second! Multiply the full wavelength in meters by 2,450,000,000 waves/second to get the speed of light. You should get something close to 300,000,000 meters/second.

What's Happening?

Your microwave oven heats food by using light waves. Light is simply a form of energy, and when microwave light hits your food, that energy is converted from light into heat. Most microwaves have a plate that spins around to help the light waves heat your food evenly, but when we take it out, the light waves only heat the food where they pass through the food. This allows you to measure the wavelength of the light in your microwave, which can be used to calculate its speed.

What If?

What if you use other foods for this experiment? Try a tray full of marshmallows or bread with butter.

Does it matter how high up off the bottom of the microwave you place the food? Put a microwave-safe bowl upside down and put your plate of chocolate on top of that. Do you get better results?

Metamerism Matters

Have you ever put on a pair of socks that looked the same color, only to go out in the sunshine and discover that one is black and one is blue? When the light changes how you see the color of your socks, you have metamerism!

Do It!

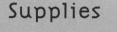

Supplies

Shoebox,
Flashlight,
Scissors, Balloons
of different colors,
Small objects of
different colors
(plastic brick toys
work well), Tape

1. Cut a hole in the center of the lid of the shoebox that is the same size as the top of the flashlight. Cut a 1-inch square hole on a short end of the shoebox.

2. Put a red object in the box. Turn on the flashlight and shine it in the hole on top. Look through the small hole on the side. What color is the object?

3. Cut the bottom off a blue balloon and stretch it over the flashlight. Shine the blue light in the hole on top of the box and look in the small hole in the side. What color is the object now? Try other combinations of object and light colors. Does the color of an object depend on the color of light you use?

What's Happening?

When you look at an object, the color you see depends on the color reflected off the object. So, a red object reflects red light but absorbs all the other colors. If you look at a red object with a blue light, it will appear black. All the blue light is absorbed and there is no red light to reflect to your eye.

What If?

What if you use different "white" lights to look at the objects? Try bright sunlight, fluorescent lights, incandescent lights, and LED lights. Do the colors change? What if you test your black and blue socks? What kind of light makes them both look blue or both look black?

Kaleidoscope

Kaleidoscope means "beautiful shape" in Greek. What beautiful shapes will you see in yours?

Supplies

Paper towel tube; Cardboard; Aluminum foil; Scissors; Ruler; Tape; Markers, paint, stickers (optional)

Do It!

1. Cut three pieces of cardboard 1 inch wide and as long as your paper towel tube. Wrap each piece with foil, shiny side out and as smooth as possible.
2. Assemble the mirrors into a long triangle tube and tape them together. Slide the triangle tube into the paper towel tube and tape it down. Make sure you can still see through both ends. Decorate the tube with markers, paint, and stickers, if you like.
3. Look into the tube and point the other end at different objects. What do you see?

What's Happening?

Look at yourself in the mirror. What do you see? Light reflects to create an image. Turn your back to the mirror and use a handheld mirror to look behind you into the mirror. What do you see now? The mirrors reflect back and forth until the image becomes too small to see. This is what happens in the kaleidoscope, but with three mirrors, the pattern gets more interesting.

Rainbow Paper

Capture a rainbow on paper and hang it on the wall!

Supplies

Clear nail polish, Black paper, Scissors, Shallow pan, Warm water

Do It!

1. Pour 1 inch of warm water into the pan.
2. Cut a piece of black paper smaller than the pan. Place the paper into the water.
3. Pour three drops of clear nail polish onto the water. Lift the paper by its corners straight up so that the nail polish stays on the paper. Lay the paper flat and let it dry for 10 minutes. Tilt the dry paper as you look at it. Can you see the rainbow?

What's Happening?

The color of light can be described by its wavelength. Visible light with large wavelengths are red, orange, and yellow; short wavelengths are green, blue, and indigo. The nail polish forms a film on the paper that's so thin that the light reflecting off it and the light reflecting off the bottom of the film combine. Some colors in the light combine, and the color appears twice as bright. Other colors combine, the waves cancel out, and the color does not appear at all. All of this combining creates a rainbow of colors.

Sky Colors

Why is the sky blue and sunset orange?

Supplies

Clear, straight drinking glass; Water; Milk; Measuring spoon; Flashlight; Tabletop in a dark room

= Do It! =

1. Fill the glass with water and add 2 teaspoons of milk.
2. Shine the flashlight through the glass. Look at the milky water on the side next to the flashlight. The water appears blue! Look at the water on the opposite side of the flashlight. The water looks orange!

What's Happening?

When light shines through the sky, it bounces off tiny particles. Scientists call this scattering. The milky water acts like particles in the atmosphere. The light with the shortest wavelength (blue) is scattered the most. This is the color we see when the sun is high in the sky. When you look at the milky water from the side, you see scattered blue light.

At sunset, the sun is low and the sunlight travels through more atmosphere. By the time the sunlight reaches your eyes, the blue is scattered out. When you look at the water opposite the flashlight, you see the orange light with the blue scattered out.

Un-mixing Colors

With this experiment, you get to turn back time!

= Do It! =

Supplies

Large clear glass, Small clear glass, Corn syrup, Water, 3 droppers, 3 small cups, Food coloring, 3 spoons, 4 large binder clips

1. Stir some corn syrup and a different color of food coloring together into each small cup.
2. Fill the large glass ⅓ full of corn syrup. Place the small glass inside and push it into the corn syrup. Fill the small glass with water. Clip the binder clips on the large glass to hold the center glass in place.
3. Place a large drop of each colored syrup into the syrup between the two glasses.
4. Hold the large glass, and then very slowly turn the small glass. The colored drops will appear to mix with the syrup. Turn the glass until the colors have gone all the way around. Then slowly turn the inside glass in the other direction. Watch the colored drops un-mix!

What's Happening?

When you have a dense and slow-moving liquid, such as corn syrup, and you mix it slowly, then it has what scientists call laminar flow. These liquids don't actually mix. Instead, many thin, parallel layers move around the glass. When you turn the glass the other direction, the color drops stay in their layers and come back together.

Index